WIN!

Also by Dan Strutzel and Traci Shoblom

The Power of Charisma

The Power of Positive Selling

The Growth Mindset

WIN!

Positive Negotiating *and* Decision Making *for the* Real World

DAN STRUTZEL *and*
TRACI SHOBLOM

MEDIA

Published 2023 by Gildan Media LLC
aka G&D Media
www.GandDmedia.com

Cover design by Tom McKeveny

Interior design by Meghan Day Healey of Story Horse, LLC

Library of Congress Cataloging-in-Publication Data is available upon request

ISBN: 978-1-7225-0632-2

10   9   8   7   6   5   4   3   2   1

INTRODUCTION
Life Is a Series of Negotiations

"Mommy, can I have some chips?" Eight-year-old Madison was in the kitchen with her mother one evening, helping her make dinner.

"No, sweetheart. It's too close to dinnertime. It will ruin your appetite."

Ever the negotiator, Madison replied, "Just one handful?"

"No, honey."

"Five chips. Can I have five chips?"

"No, Madison."

"One chip. Can I have one chip?"

Laughing, her mother replied, "No. You may not eat even one chip."

"Can I lick a chip?" This was one persistent girl.

Laughing even harder at her daughter's negotiating skills, Madison's mother held firm. "No, you may not lick a chip."

Refusing to quit until she won something, Madison asked, "Well, can I think about chips?"

"Yes, Madison. You can think about chips."

Happy with her "win," Madison sat on the dining room chair with her eyes closed, thinking about chips until dinner was ready.

The fact is all of life is a series of negotiations. From an early age, we learn how to get what we want by negotiating for it. Whether we're getting a toy or a present we want as a child to getting a raise or extra foam on our lattes as adults, negotiation is always with us.

The process is not as cold as it sounds. Negotiation, as we are using the term here, is simply the process of creating an agreement that is an acceptable outcome for everyone—a common ground. Of course, not all negotiation results in an agreement, nor does all negotiation result in an outcome that works best for everyone. In fact, not every person negotiating *wants* to come to agreement or find an outcome that is best for the other party (some people want to win at all costs). But for the purposes of this book, we're establishing the ideal that negotiation is the process of creating an agreement that is an acceptable outcome for everybody.

Negotiation is the process of creating an agreement that is an acceptable outcome for everybody.

Let's break that down a little further to help us understand the nuances of negotiation.

Process: Negotiation is a process. This means that one must take certain steps to get from Point A (no agreed-upon acceptable outcome) to Point B (an agreed-upon acceptable outcome). You'll find many processes for negotiating, and this book will teach you an easy and effective one.

Creating an agreement: An important element in effective negotiation is creating agreement among the different parties. If Madison, in our earlier example, had just given up when her mother said no to eating chips, then there would have been no agreement. The same would have been true if Mom had just said no to every solution that her daughter offered, without accepting one of them ("thinking about chips"). For the outcome to be truly an effect of negotiation, there must be some form of agreement.

An acceptable outcome: This is not the same thing as the best solution or ideal outcome. When a couple is getting divorced, for example, often compromises have to be made for the parties to come to an agreement. Ideally, each party would get exactly what he or she wanted (she gets the house because he doesn't want it; he gets the car because she doesn't want it). This ideal outcome actually doesn't require negotiation. In negotiation, one must often trade something one wants less for something one wants more. Sometimes, as was the case with Madison, what you want the most is to know that you've "won." It's key to note that we are defining negotiation as a *process*, and that is different from an *outcome*. This book is designed to teach you a process that will increase the odds of a successful outcome.

For everybody: This is important. It's not negotiation if the outcome isn't truly an outcome that is acceptable to all parties. If one party feels cheated, coerced, or taken advantage of, it's not negotiation, it's manipulation. That's not what we're going for here.

Negotiation, Influence, and Persuasion— They're Not the Same

Many people use the terms *negotiation*, *influence*, and *persuasion* interchangeably But there are subtle differences. Janet Cropper, founder of NoLimits Coaching, cites these dictionary definitions for the terms:

- Persuade: "induce someone to do something through reasoning or argument"
- Negotiate: "discuss something formally in order to create an agreement"
- Influence: "the power to change or affect someone or something without directly forcing it to happen and without apparent effort"

Going back to our story, if Madison had tried to reason with her mother by sharing all the reasons why she should be allowed to eat chips, she would be engaging in *persuasion*. If she had simply set the bag of chips on the counter in an effort to get her mother to notice them and offer chips as a before-dinner snack, that would have been *influence*. But, in her case, she discussed eating chips in an effort to gain agreement that she could eat them. That's *negotiation*.

What Can Becoming a Better Negotiator Do for You?

While there are elements of influence and persuasion that go into negotiating, this book is focused on a specific process that can help you become a better negotiator in every area of your life. Here are just a few of the outcomes that effective negotiation skills can bring about.

- Better relationships
- Getting into better schools and jobs
- Higher income
- Improved self-image
- Helping others get more of what they want

As we've discovered, negotiation is a core element of human interaction. From the bedroom to the boardroom, the principles of negotiation are at the foundation of our society. Are you ready to learn how to have a winning mindset?

Part I

How People Make Decisions

Understanding how people make decisions will make you a better negotiator.

1

Three Factors That Influence Decisions

At 6:00 a.m. Mike rolls over and hits the snooze button on his alarm. This has become his routine—delaying the inevitable start to his workday. When he first took the job at Trynotec five years ago, he'd been excited at the prospect of moving up in the company and having work that stimulated him as well as a supportive environment. Unfortunately, the job turned out to provide none of those things.

Six months ago, Mike's precarious work situation came to a head when Trynotec was bought out by a larger company in the same industry. Despite assurances that everything would stay in place as is, things have been starting to change. The collegial atmosphere of Trynotec transformed into a competitive, dog-eat-dog one. No one was getting promoted, and in fact there was talk about reductions in force. And don't even get him started on the work! Let's just say that it doesn't take a college graduate to do the tasks Mike spends his days doing. Mike is afraid that if he stays at Trynotec, he'll either be reduced to nothing more than a glorified technician or get stuck in the same boring job for the rest of his life. Even worse, he could get fired. With Karen pregnant again, he doesn't have enough money saved to go for long without an income.

As he lies in bed, waiting for the alarm to go off again, he wonders, "Should I stay at Trynotec and hope for the best? Should I start looking for another position? What should I do?"

As human beings, we are faced with hundreds of decisions every day ranging from small ones (what should I wear today?) to large ones (should I quit my job?). We are decision-making machines.

But most people never stop to think about how we make decisions. Although this is not one of the many books that delve deeply into the area of decision-making, understanding how we make decisions can help us become better negotiators. After all, if you understand how the other person's mind works, you're more likely to come up with a solution that appeals to them.

Mann, This Is a Tough Decision

In 1977, Irving Janis and Leon Mann proposed a descriptive model of the decision-making process in their book, *Decision Making: A Psychological Analysis of Conflict, Choice, and Commitment*. They said that the need to make a decision involves a conflict that creates a certain amount of stress, and that the amount of stress we experience affects whether or not we can make a good decision. The reason for this is that when we're under a lot of stress ("environmental load"), we tend to engage in unproductive information-search, assessment, and decision-making patterns.

Although you've probably never thought of it that way, you've experienced this. Recall a time when you're already late to an appointment, and suddenly you can't find your car keys. Your stress level skyrockets, and you start looking everywhere for your keys, including places that are completely unlikely ("Why would the keys be in the freezer?" "I don't know, just keep looking!"). You then start to think of different modes of transportation ("Should I just call Uber?"). Then, as you're about to call and cancel the appointment, you see the keys hanging on the hook, where they belong.

Janis and Mann say that the stress stems from two concerns—worrying about the objective personal and material losses that result from the chosen alternative ("If I keep looking for these keys, I'll miss the appointment, and they'll charge me a fee.") and worry about the subjective losses that may lower self-esteem ("What kind of idiot loses his keys like this?").

The model is called a cognitive-assessment model because we use thought processes to assess the potential outcomes of a decision. According to Janis and Mann, there are three antecedent conditions, or factors that are in place, that determine which pattern a person will use when making a decision:

1. The awareness of a serious risk if nothing is done
2. The hope of finding a better alternative

3. The belief that there is enough time to learn about and assess the situation and choose the best alternative

In the case of Mike in our opening story, he is aware that there is a serious risk if he doesn't do anything. He could get fired or become stuck in a job he hates for years to come. He does have hopes of finding a better alternative. And, because the talk of downsizing is still just talk, he believes he has enough time to learn about and assess the situation and find the best alternative. In other words, he still has time to look for a good job that satisfies his needs, because he hasn't been fired yet.

But let's say, for the purposes of discussion, that the factors are different. What if Mike really doesn't think about the risks at this point? What if he doesn't truly believe that getting fired is a realistic possibility? Then he's not going to be motivated to make a decision because he's not aware that there is a serious risk if he doesn't.

What if he has no hope for a better alternative? What if the industry he is in is so competitive that he would need to go back to school or choose a different career altogether?

Or what if he doesn't actually have enough time to assess the situation and make a good choice? What if, instead, Mike has been let go, with two months' severance pay? He won't have the luxury of spending months on a job search, but will feel pressured to take the first job that he is offered.

The Three Factors and Negotiating

Let's look at what the three factors—Janis and Mann's antecedent conditions—have to do with negotiating. What if we were Mike's manager, and we didn't want him to leave? How would the three factors affect how we interact with him? Bear in mind that this is not part of the negotiation process that we'll learn in a later section of the book. It's simply examining the factors that would lead Mike to making a decision that would require negotiating later on.

1. The awareness of a serious risk if nothing is done

If we were Mike's manager, and we don't want him to start looking for another job, either we would make sure that Mike is unaware of the risk or we would downplay its severity: "Mike, all that talk of reduction in force is coming from the old-timers. No one with any credibility is actually saying that. This is just an adjustment period." This isn't to say that we would lie. But if the situation is still ambiguous, then we can play to the ambiguity: "No one really knows what's going to happen yet."

2. The hope of finding a better alternative

Another option is to reduce Mike's hope of finding a better alternative: "You know how tough the job market is out there. When Carl left last year, we had a flood of applicants trying to get his job. I, for one, would not want to be job hunting in this economy. Who knows what kind of job I'd have to take?"

3. The belief that there is enough time to learn about and assess the situation and choose the best alternative

Finally, we might play the "time card." In this case, it means influencing Mike to realize that there is plenty of time later on to make those kinds of decisions and that the best alternative for Mike is to wait and see.

In another scenario, though, we might emphasize that time is running out and that a decision needs to be made quickly. This happens a lot in sales: "The special price is only valid if you purchase it this weekend."

As you're reading this, reflect on your own experience. Think about a time when you had to make a decision. How did the three factors set the stage for how you made it? It's easy to see that we make different decisions depending on the environment we are in. When we have all the time and options in the world available to us, we use a different process than if we're under stress and time pressure.

This chapter has looked at three factors that come into play when a person is facing a decision and how those factors determine what kind of process they'll use. We then looked at how those three factors play into negotiation, because if you're able to understand where the other party's thoughts are, you can better tailor your negotiating strategy to meet them.

In the next chapter, we'll look more closely at the patterns of decision-making, so that when you are negotiating, you can use that awareness to influence the outcome.

2

Five Basic Patterns
Of Decision-Making

Harold and Maureen have been married for sixty years, most of which were spent raising their five kids in a beautiful, sprawling farmhouse. The whole family has incredible memories of birthdays, graduations, weddings, holidays, and other meaningful life experiences here.

But the time has come for Harold and Maureen to downsize, and they want to sell the house and buy a condo in Florida. To prevent any conflict over which of the kids was told what, and when, they decide to write everyone a group email giving them the news that the house will be going on the market at the end of the month.

As is common in families, each of the five adult children has a different pattern of decision-making, and therefore reacts differently upon getting the email.

The youngest son, Luke, pretty much ignores the issue. He's got a lot going on at work and is moving into a new apartment himself. So he just marks the email as unread and saves it for later.

Mary's pattern of decision-making is to not question it much. She tells her husband, "Well, if that's what they want to do, who am I to challenge it? I guess we'll be vacationing in Florida from now on."

Laura has always been a bit of a dreamer, and this issue is no exception. As she's reading the email, she thinks, "I can't really deal with this right now. Maybe they'll change their mind. I'll talk to the others about it the next time we have a family Zoom session."

Hannah, the oldest daughter, immediately goes into a panic. "They can't do this! There has to be another solution. I know. Maybe we can all take turns living with Mom and Dad for part of the year. If everyone lived there for a couple of months, then Mom and Dad wouldn't have to be alone, and we wouldn't have to sell the house."

Only the eldest son, Brian, approaches the news rationally. He takes a look at the factors, such as the cost of living in Florida, the feasibility of a reverse mortgage, and the possibility that all of the children could buy into the house jointly, allowing Mom and Dad to move to Florida without having to sell it. After doing more research, Brian begins to compose a reply to his parents and siblings, offering a solution.

This scenario is a common one in groups of all kinds. Individuals have different ways of making decisions, and it can affect the negotiating process when these patterns clash. In the story, even though each child wants the same thing— to relieve their parents of the burden of caring for a large property—their different patterns of decision-making lead them to very different behaviors.

In their book, *Decision Making*, researchers Janis and Mann outline five patterns of coping with stressful decisions:

- **Unconflicted adherence:** The person ignores the decision.
- **Unconflicted change:** The person does not question the decision about the new, recommended course of action.
- **Defensive avoidance:** The person procrastinates, shifts responsibility, and may engage in wishful thinking.
- **Hypervigilance or "panic mode":** The decision-maker, as Janis and Mann say, "searches frantically for a way out of the dilemma and impulsively seizes upon a hastily contrived solution that seems to promise immediate relief, overlooking the full range of consequences of his choice."
- **Vigilance:** The person searches carefully for relevant information, remaining unbiased when searching and evaluating the alternatives carefully before making a decision.

In our scenario about their parents, each of the children represents one of the five patterns.

- **Unconflicted adherence:** By not even reading the email and saving it for later, Luke doesn't have any internal conflict with it. "It's not a problem until I actually deal with it, right?"
- **Unconflicted change:** Mary just figures, "Hey. Things change. Life goes on." She doesn't have any inner conflict about the change. Sure, she's a little sad, but she's okay with her parents' decision.
- **Defensive avoidance:** Because Laura lives so much in her head, it's easy for her to avoid dealing with the decision. She spends her time hoping the problem will go away, wishing

that things were different and they were all still kids living at home. So Laura pretty much avoids dealing with it at all.

- **Hypervigilance:** Clearly Hannah was in a panic when she came up with the crazy idea of having each of the adult children move back to the family home, with their own kids and spouses, for part of every year. She clearly didn't think it through. But the idea of her parents selling the family home is so awful that she knows she had to come up with some solution, no matter how farfetched.
- **Vigilance:** Brian is the one person in the family who is being vigilant in his decision-making. He's taking the time to research the options in an unbiased way, and then to come up with a recommended course of action for his parents and siblings.

Janis and Mann demonstrated, using the results of research experiments, that each particular pattern leads to a different way of processing information. Both *unconflicted adherence* and *unconflicted change* lead to a low level of interest in information about the issue, whether pro or con. Luke and Mary don't really spend a lot of mental energy dealing with it. *Defensive avoidance* will lead to selective exposure to information that affirms the decision-maker's choice. This means that Laura is only going to pay attention to the information that leads her to believe that her parents won't sell their house. Chances are, she'll be blindsided if they really do move to Florida: "I never thought they would really do it!"

Hypervigilance will lead to a high level of interest in all information, even if it is irrelevant. Hannah is likely to stay up late at night reading everything she can on retiring to Florida, even to the point of watching YouTube videos of retirees playing golf.

Vigilance, however, should lead decision-makers to consider relevant information on all sides of the issue. So although Brian doesn't really want his parents to sell the house, if it makes the best sense to do that, he's not going to close his mind, even after he's made a recommendation to the family.

Janis and Mann put it this way: "When the conditions that favor vigilance are present, decision-makers will be open-minded in exposing themselves to information after (as well as before) they make a choice."

The Five Patterns and Negotiation

How, then, do these patterns relate to negotiation? In two ways. First, it's clear that vigilance is the ideal pattern for negotiating because your mind stays open to gathering the kind of information you need at the negotiating table. You won't allow yourself to fall into some of the common decision traps that people tend to fall into (more on that in a moment).

Second, if you're able to identify the decision pattern of the other party, you're better able to deal with it in your negotiation. For example, if you're negotiating with someone who is being hypervigilant, you can work to reduce the state of panic so that they can calm down and see that what you're proposing is to their benefit. Alternatively, you can allow them to continue to operate from a panicked emotional state and use that to your strategic advantage.

Here is more about negotiating with the different types of decision patterns.

- **Unconflicted adherence:** With a person using this pattern, you want to help them to understand the importance of the situation. Remember that this pattern is indicated by someone ignoring the decision. They just don't see it as important. So your job is to help them to see that the issue being negotiated is important.
- **Unconflicted change:** When negotiating with a person using this pattern, you can use it to your advantage because they'll be more likely to accept your proposed outcome. This pattern is typified by a "I'm cool with whatever decision we make" attitude.
- **Defensive avoidance:** A person using the defensive-avoidance pattern is likely to be the toughest one to negotiate with, because they'll want to put off making a commitment for as long as possible. They'll use clever tactics to avoid negotiating with you, such as canceling appointments, needing additional "research" (this is different from the research done by a person using the vigilance pattern), and postponing any actions on their part. Understanding the pattern and expecting it can go a long way in negotiating with a person using defensive avoidance.
- **Hypervigilance:** A person in a hypervigilant state is experiencing heightened emotions, which causes them to frantically seek options. You can either calm them down so that they move into vigilance, or use their emotional imbalance as a strategic advantage, depending on what is best for the situation.

Help, I'm Trapped in a Bad Decision!

As mentioned, we tend to fall into some decision traps when we're making tough choices. Here are ten of them, based on the research by Edward J. Russo and Paul J. H. Shoemaker.* When we are falling into one of the dysfunctional decision patterns described in this scenario, we tend to fall into one or more of these decision traps.

1. **Plunging in:** This is just what it sounds like. You make a decision without fully gathering information or thinking the outcome through. And you often come to regret it.

2. **Frame blindness:** You are focused on the wrong problem because of the way you are framing the situation. One example would be a company that is focused on developing a new and improved DVD player, when in reality fewer and fewer people are using DVDs.

3. **Lack of frame control:** Failing to consciously define the problem in more ways than one or being unduly influenced by others.

4. **Overconfidence in your judgment:** Failing to collect key factual information because you are too sure of your assumptions and opinions.

---

* Edward J. Russo and Paul J. H. Schoemaker, *Decision Traps: The Ten Barriers to Brilliant Decision-making and How to Overcome Them* (New York: Doubleday, 1989).

5. **Shortsighted shortcuts:** Relying inappropriately on rules of thumb, such as implicitly trusting the most readily available information or giving undue weight to convenient facts.

6. **Shooting from the hip:** This, too, is just what it sounds like. It's making decisions based on the belief that you can keep all of the relevant information in your head instead of using a systematic process to evaluate the different options.

7. **Group failure:** Assuming that with many smart people involved, good choices will follow automatically, and therefore you fail to manage the group decision-making process.

8. **Fooling yourself about feedback**: We've all fallen victim to this at one point or another. Either we don't believe what someone tells us because we don't want to hear it and so convince ourselves that the feedback is wrong, or we believe false feedback because it agrees with what we want to hear. This can cause us to search and search for feedback until we find what we want to hear, regardless of how reliable the source.

9. **Not keeping track:** Assuming that experience will make its lessons available automatically, and therefore failing to keep systematic records to track the results of your decisions and failing to analyze these results in ways that reveal their key lessons.

10. **Failure to audit your decision process:** When someone doesn't think about how they are making decisions, which, of course is not you, because you're reading this chapter.

In this chapter we have delved into some of the flawed processes that people use when making decisions, as well as some of the traps that we fall in. Surely you can find examples of times when you've used each of the processes and fallen into these traps. It's human nature.

But in successful negotiation, it's wise to stay vigilant, so that you can both avoid falling into decision traps and keep the upper hand at the negotiating table. If you can see that the other party is falling into a decision trap, you'll be able to use vigilance to better your chances of getting the outcome you want.

In the next chapter, we'll look at some of the special circumstances that affect decision-making: conflict, stress, and time constraints. These relevant factors influence how people negotiate.

3

Special Circumstances

"Hey, can you both come in my office for a minute?" John is the creative director of an advertising agency, and his two best people are putting together a presentation for a potential new account. It's a big client and would mean a lot of revenue for the agency.

Mike and Abby look at each other skeptically as they walk into John's office. "What's up, boss?"

"Well, I've got some good news and bad news about the Brix account. The good news is that the CEO is interested in what we do and wants to sit in on the presentation. The bad news is that they now want to do it next week instead of next month. I hate to dump this on you guys like this, and it's still really important that we do our best work. I know you have a lot of other accounts you're working on, and if you want me to put Tom and Lynne on this, I can."

Wisely, Mike and Abby project confidence they don't feel. "No, Mike. We got this. No problem."

The tune changes, though, once they get back to Abby's office. Mike immediately begins to panic. "There is no way we can be ready in a week. We haven't even gotten the concept yet, let alone do the mock-up or get the art. We were going to produce an animated video! All that's out the window now. We might as well just walk in there wearing sweatpants and sketch our ideas out on a whiteboard. We're never going to get this account now."

Abby gets mad. "Well, with that attitude, you're right. I hate how you always do this. You immediately go negative. How about maybe seeing this as a challenge? It may not be perfect, but it will be good enough. I can sit down right now and open up a presentation and put together something presentable for the client. Sure, I won't have enough time for a sophisticated multimedia presentation, but just because we don't have weeks to analyze and perfect every little detail doesn't mean we won't land the account. Would you like me to see if John can put Tom in instead? I'm sure Lynne would be happy to work with you on her accounts, and I'd be working with someone who has a little bit of faith in our agency . . . and in me."

In a perfect world, we would all make decisions in a calm, rational manner, with all the time in the world and unlimited information so that decision-making would be stress-free. But that's not the world we live in. In the real world, we often find ourselves making decisions with limited information and time, and with competing interests. It causes stress. And the more stress we have, the less we're able to make good decisions. It becomes a vicious cycle.

This idea isn't new but has been around for a long time. In 1955 Herb Simon challenged the then-current view of decision-making. This traditional model asserted that when people make decisions, they try to get the best possible outcome. It's called *optimizing*. In order to do this, though, Simon made five assumptions about the decision-maker*:

1. Has full knowledge of relevant aspects of the environment, including alternatives, events (states of nature), the probabilities of those events, and the outcomes associated with combinations of alternatives and events,

2. Possesses a well-organized and stable set of preferences,

3. Enjoys superb computational abilities that are capable of optimization,

4. Is capable of cool decision-making, is not swayed by emotions or stress, and

5. Has immediate access to free information.

Just reading that, you can tell that Simon's assumptions in no way reflect the way we make decisions in the real world. So Simon came up with a new framework that more accurately reflects the way we humans actually make decisions. He called it the *new rationality*. In this new rationality,

• The classical view of rationality is replaced with bounded rationality in which the decision-maker tries to find satisfactory solutions within many cognitive, perceptual, situational, and other bounds.

---

* Simon, Herbert A. (1955) "A behavioral model of rational choice," *The Quarterly Journal of Economics*, vol. 69, n. 1, February: 99–118, compiled in, and quoted from, Simon (1957: 241–260).

• Aspiration levels are important and dynamic. Success and failure may result in changing levels of aspiration and thus in changes in what is deemed acceptable or unacceptable.

• Information acquisition and processing are time-consuming, laborious, and costly. Thus the best level of persistence in pursuit of a goal involves a tradeoff between the potential costs and benefits of search.

• Preferences are fluid. For example, preferences may change with time and maturation. In addition, consequences may change one's payoff function. And, of course, we may simply not know our preferences because of lack of experience (and a corresponding reluctance to explore alternatives).

Therefore Simon proposed that we humans make decisions that *satisfice* instead of optimize. In other words, we do the best we can given the constraints. Of course, the fact that we can't always optimize doesn't mean that some people still don't try. Those people are what Simon called *maximizers*.

Maximizers seek to determine the best possible alternative; satisficers seek the first acceptable alternative in the set.

You've likely experienced that yourself. You're going out to dinner with some friends, and they've left it up to you to choose the restaurant. If you were optimizing, you'd choose the best restaurant in town—the one right on the beach. But it's expensive, and your friends are all on a budget. And Julie is a vegan, so you need a place that serves vegan-friendly food. And because Glenn has kids, it has to be on a Friday, after work but not too late.

You go online to find a place, and there are dozens of possible choices. But you can't spend all day analyzing the menus of every one, so you choose the pasta place that's centrally located, reasonably priced, has vegan options, and is open early on Friday. Sure, there might be a better option, but you satisfice and take the first one that meets all of your criteria.

Maximizers seek to determine the best possible alternative. Satisficers seek the first acceptable alternative in the set.

Clearly people differ widely in the amount of information they use in decision-making. Some people reach conclusions on the basis of just a few facts. Others reach conclusions only after gathering and studying large amounts of information.

Satisficers use a few pieces of information to come up with a decision that is good enough. Maximizers consider a lot of information before making a decision.

One particular framework for identifying decision styles is based upon a conceptual model originally developed by Michael J. Driver and then further defined by Driver and Kenneth Brousseau. It's called the driver decision style model and explores how people make decisions on the basis of two factors—the amount of information they use when making decisions, and how many alternatives they consider when making a decision.

According to Driver and Brousseau, "Satisficers know that there is more information that they could take into consideration, and their tendency is to want to get on with things. They prefer to keep moving, rather than 'analyzing things to death.' At the other extreme is the maximizer mode. Maximizers want to be sure that they have considered all of the relevant facts, and that they have missed no important details, no matter how subtle. Their interest is in coming up with a high quality solution or in learning something new and important."

Now let's recall a conversation between a maximizer and a satisficer whom we've already met, although we didn't know the terminology—Mike and Abby from the opening scenario.

The tune changes about the impending project management once they get back to Abby's office. Mike immediately begins to panic, and you will recall he says, "There is no way we can be ready in a week. We haven't even gotten the concept yet, let alone do the mock-up or get the art. We were going to produce an animated video! All that's out the window now. We might as well just walk in there wearing sweatpants and sketch our ideas out on a whiteboard. We're never going to get this account now."

Abby gets mad. "Well, with that attitude, you're right. I hate how you always do this. You immediately go negative. How about maybe seeing this as a challenge? It may not be perfect, but it will be good enough. I can sit down right now and open up a presentation and put together something presentable for the client. Sure, I won't have enough time for a sophisticated multimedia presentation, but just because we don't have weeks to analyze and perfect every little detail doesn't mean we won't land the account. Would you like me to see if John can put Tom in instead? I'm sure Lynne would be happy to work with you on her accounts, and I'd be working with someone who has a little bit of faith in our agency . . . and in me."

Now we can clearly see that Mike is a maximizer and Abby is a satisficer. We also can tell from what we learned in the previous chapter that Mike has gone into hypervigilance and is panicking.

Let's take a look at the four components of the new rationality as they apply to Mike and Abby.

1. The classical view of rationality is replaced with bounded rationality, in which the decision-maker tries to find satisfactory solutions within many cognitive, perceptual, situational, and other bounds.

    In other words, Mike and Abby have restrictions now, as they only have a week to prepare the presentation. Their decisions about the campaign will be made with bounded rationality as a result.

2. Aspiration levels are important and dynamic. Success and failure may result in changing levels of aspiration and thus in changes in what is deemed acceptable or unacceptable.

    Mike and Abby originally had high aspirations for what they considered a successful presentation. But, given the constraints, what they might have considered a failure before might be considered a success now.

3. Information acquisition and processing are time-consuming, laborious, and costly. Thus the best level of persistence in

pursuit of a goal involves a tradeoff between the potential costs and benefits of search.

Mike and Abby don't have the time now to do as much research on the ad campaign as they would have otherwise had. They could theoretically hire a team of researchers to do it for them, but it would cost too much.

4. Preferences are fluid. For example, preferences may change with time and maturation. In addition, consequences may change one's payoff function. And, of course, we may simply not know our preferences because of lack of experience (and a corresponding reluctance to explore alternatives).

Abby would prefer to work with Mike on the project. But if the consequence of working with him is that she has a partner with no faith in her, then her preference for that could change.

Satisficing, Maximizing, Negotiating

So, then, how would a satisficer and a maximizer negotiate together? Here are some tips for negotiating with each style.

Tips on Negotiating with a Satisficer

Bear in mind that at some point, we all become satisficers, because there is no optimal environment for making decisions. Nevertheless, if the person on the opposite end of the table has a natural tendency toward satisficing, you can use that to your advantage. Remember that they tend to get overwhelmed with too much information and too many choices.

So you can either (a) give them a huge volume of information and a large number of choices, and then present your solution as the most optimal one, or (b) pare down the information and present your outcome as the one that satisfies as many of their conditions as possible. In other words, you want to craft the negotiation so that your outcome is the first one that is "good enough."

Tips If You're the Satisficer

The following is excerpted from an article that appeared in the Daily Blog on Negotiation from Harvard Law School.*

When it comes to negotiation, an excess of choices can not only be overwhelming but also can blind you to a good offer. The owner of a midsized business who deliberated too long about whether to (1) accept a large chain's buyout offer, (2) partner with another midsized firm, or (3) keep his business independent found his negotiation position considerably weakened when the chain decided to buy out his competitor instead.

The point of the negotiation is not to win, but to achieve a deal that is good enough. Negotiators who satisfice don't haggle over every last penny. With clear objectives you can achieve a deal that satisfies those objectives.

On the same note, when satisficing, be careful letting your counterpart know your bottom-line, highest price, or lowest acceptable bid. This is an example of the anchoring effect in negotiation and demonstrates the powerful effect of information on bargaining strategy.

---

* Susan Hackley, "Satisficing and Negotiation," Daily Blog on Negotiation, Harvard Law School, June 29, 2017; https://www.pon.harvard.edu/daily/business-negotiations/satisficing-and-negotiation/.

The prospect of sharing information with a negotiating counterpart can be scary—it can fix your counterpart into a position at the negotiation table you didn't intend (an example of the anchoring effect). Share too much, and the other side might conclude that you're desperate to make a deal, any deal. There's also the risk of giving away privileged information that your counterpart could use against you. A careful analysis of the pros and cons of sharing information in negotiation will help you approach negotiation scenarios with a greater sense of confidence and security.

Don't wait for the other side to open up to you first. The advantages of sharing information during negotiation have been well documented. Thanks to the power of reciprocity, your counterpart is likely to match any information you share with valuable information of their own.

In general, you should feel comfortable revealing information about your interests in the negotiation, as well as your priorities across different issues. That doesn't mean that if there are five issues on the table, you should reveal that you care about only two of them. Rather, stress that all the issues are important to you, but you'd have a hard time budging on two of them.

Tips on Negotiating with a Maximizer

If you're negotiating with a maximizer, the key to success is to understand that they are likely to want a lot of information and many different options so that they can come up with the "best" solution. For them, time or expense or effort can pale in comparison to the idea of getting the perfect outcome.

This means that you'll want to create as many variations on what you want as possible in order to increase the chances that the other party will agree to one of them. Be aware of their tendency to take a lot of time, and, if needed, you can create a time constraint to move them toward hypervigilance. This might cause the maximizer to narrow down the choices and be willing to satisfice.

Tips If You're the Maximizer

If you're the one who is the maximizer, be aware of your tendency to overanalyze the situation. Studies show that satisficers end up happier with their outcomes than do maximizers. Another article from Harvard's Daily Blog on Negotiation says this*:

> Psychologically driven to seek the best possible outcome, these perfectionists [maximizers] leave no stone unturned when preparing for talks. In the process, maximizers waste time, and their goals often come at a high economic and emotional cost. Furthermore, maximizers' abstract judgments prior to negotiation may not match their real-world choices. . . .
>
> This research suggests two lessons for negotiation preparation. First, when setting goals, "don't let the perfect be the enemy of the good." Weighing countless options costs time and money. Second, treat your goals and tradeoffs as provisional starting points. You can update your preferences and options as they emerge during the negotiation.

---

* Pon Staff, "Dealing with Choice Overload," Daily Blog on Negotiation, Harvard Law School, Oct. 14, 2009; https://www.pon.harvard.edu/daily/negotiation-skills-daily/dealing-with-choice -overload/. Adapted from "Too Much of a Good Thing? The Role of Choice in Negotiation" by Michael Wheeler, professor, Harvard Business School. In *Negotiation* 7, no. 9 (September 2004).

Stress and Decision-Making

In our earlier example, Mike and Abby both experienced stress when told that they were going to have to give their presentation several weeks earlier than planned. This led to conflict and variations in how they reacted to that stress.

When humans perceive a threat, it activates the sympathetic nervous system, which causes the heart rate to increase, the blood pressure to rise, and the amount of information we take in to diminish. Our bodies prepare for fight or flight. In other words, we assess the situation and decide if we are going to run away (if a bear is chasing us, for example) or fight (if we are being attacked by a mosquito, we're likely to swat it). In some cases, though, individuals just give up, because they've learned over time that fighting or fleeing has little effect on the outcome.

So when Mike and Abby got back to her office, the stress caused them each to react differently, as a result of their personal histories. Mike panicked and wanted to retreat and give up. Abby went into fight mode and wanted to win.

Because of their different reactions to stress, they each made different decisions about the course of action to take. Those differing reactions led them to have conflict: "Maybe I should just get someone else to work with me."

In the next chapter, we'll take a look at what happens to decision-making when two people have a conflict of interest.

4

Conflict Styles

Max and Bayne, like many twin brothers, have been competitive all of their lives. From their earliest games of Go Fish until their most recent attempt at bass fishing, the two young men have been chasing the title of "Better Brother."

When the brothers were twenty, Max fell in love with a girl named Evyn. Bayne was happy for his brother, but was also a little unhappy because of the distraction she provided for Max. Instead of running every morning, Max was meeting Evyn for coffee and croissants. Instead of hiking on the weekends, Max was drinking wine and going antique shopping. Frankly, Max was getting a little pudgy. So when Max invited Evyn to their annual RacquetBattle competition, Bayne was happy to have the advantage. He could just see the trophy on his shelf for the next year.

Max and Bayne would play five games of racquetball, and whoever won three games was declared that year's Racquet-Master. On the day of the games, Evyn and Max showed up together, kissing and hugging and holding hands.

In the locker room, Max approached his brother with a request. "Dude, I know that we usually fight hard for the win in these games, but I was wondering if you could cut me some slack today, with Evyn being here and all. We both know you could kick my butt if you wanted to. Maybe just do your brother a solid?"

Bayne's first reaction was, "No way, man. This is Racquet-Master 2022. Not my fault you've been snarfing down cheeseburgers with your girl while I've been hitting the gym. Sorry, man. You snooze, you lose."

But as Bayne walked out onto the court, he could see Evyn there, being supportive. Let's just say there wasn't anyone there rooting for Bayne. And Bayne couldn't help it, but he thought it was pretty cute that she was wearing a T-shirt with Max's face on it. They were such an adorable couple. And he was happy for his brother. He started to feel a little bad about the obvious advantage he had over Max. Would it be so wrong to play a little less hard and let his brother win in front of his girlfriend? Or should he play all-out and try to win bragging rights for the year?

In the last chapter, we took a good look at the different ways people process information when making decisions and examined how this affects negotiation. But there is another element that we haven't considered—conflict. How does the presence of conflict affect decision-making (and thereby negotiation)? And what happens if the conflict is merely inner conflict, as we are seeing in the Max and Bayne example?

As we move into the model of negotiation in Part II of this book, we'll get more into specific techniques for dealing with conflict in negotiation. For now, it's just important to understand that stress, or as we called it before, environmental load, causes some people to become more decisive and more satisficing. High environmental load can lead other people to analysis paralysis, which can lead to giving up if the person becomes too overwhelmed. Together these can lead to interpersonal conflict.

The Dual-Concern Model

Management theorists Robert Blake and Jane Mouton (1964) developed the dual-concern model, which says that individuals faced with a situation of conflict have a double interest: interest in the personal results of the conflict, or assertiveness; and interest in their relationship with the other people involved, or cooperation. So Bayne has two concerns. He wants to win the championship, but he also cares about his relationship with his brother. Attorney and mediator Don Philbin explains it this way*:

> The Dual Concern Model assumes that parties' preferred method of handling conflict is based on two underlying dimensions: assertiveness and empathy. The assertiveness dimension focuses on the degree to which one is concerned with satisfying one's own needs and interests. Conversely,

---

* Don Philbin, "Dual Concern Model," adrtoolbox blog; accessed Nov. 5, 2017; http://www.adrtoolbox.com/library/the-dual-concern-model/.

the empathy (or cooperativeness) dimension focuses on the extent to which one is concerned with satisfying the needs and interests of the other party. The intersection points of these dimensions land us in different conflict styles. It's always helpful not only to realize your own conflict style, but to appreciate the style that your opposite number is using.

The intersection points of these dimensions land us in different conflict styles. It's helpful not only to realize your own conflict style, but to identify the style that the other party is using.

A "competitive" conflict style maximizes assertiveness and minimizes empathy. Competitive types enjoy negotiation, seek to dominate and control the interaction, and tend to look at it as a game or a sport with a winner and a loser; they pay less attention to the relationship underlying the dispute since they are focused on winning and claiming the biggest piece of the pie. Competitive types approach conflict saying: "This looks like a win-lose situation, and I want to win."

An "accommodating" conflict style, in contrast, maximizes empathy and minimizes assertiveness. Accommodating types derive satisfaction from meeting the needs of others, are perceptive and intuitive about emotional states, detect subtle verbal and nonverbal cues, and tend to have good relationship building skills; they tend to deflect or give up in the face of conflict out of concern for the relationship, and tend to be vulnerable to competitive types. Accommodating types tend to believe that "[b]eing agreeable may be more important than winning."

An "avoiding" conflict style is both low in assertiveness and low in empathy. Avoiders can be adept at sidestepping pointless conflict, are able to exercise tact and diplomacy in high-conflict situations, and can artfully increase their own leverage by waiting for others to make the first concession. At the same time, however, they may "leave money on the table" and miss the opportunities for mutual gain that conflict can present, neglect underlying relationships, and allow problems to fester by ignoring them. Avoiding types worry that: "I don't want to give in, but I don't want to talk about it either."

"Collaborative" types are highly assertive and highly empathetic at the same time, therefore they are concerned about the underlying relationship and are sensitive to the other person's needs while simultaneously being committed to having their own needs met. Collaborators often see conflict as a creative opportunity and do not mind investing the time to dig deep and find a win-win solution, but may be inclined to spend more time or resources than are called for under the circumstances. Collaborative types approach conflict saying: "Let's find a way to satisfy both our goals."

Finally, a "compromising" conflict style is intermediate on both the assertiveness and empathy dimensions. Compromisers value fairness and expect to engage in some give and take when bargaining. A compromise approach allows those in conflict to take a reasonable stance that often results in an efficient resolution to the conflict. However, compromisers sometimes miss opportunities by moving too fast to split the difference, failing to search for trades and joint gains, and may neglect the relational aspects of the dispute. Compromisers approach conflict saying: "Let's meet halfway on this issue."

The model looks something like this.*

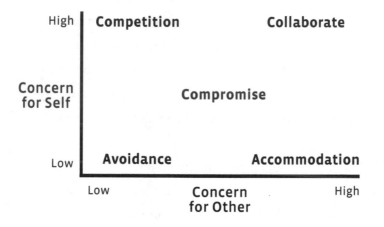

What's Your Conflict Style?

To effectively negotiate, it's a good idea to understand your dominant conflict style. Of course, we don't always use the same style, nor should we. Some circumstances call for the competitive style; whereas, others might benefit from avoidance. In other words, sometimes it's important to fight, and other times it's important to walk away. The key is in knowing the difference.

Here is a simple questionnaire that can help you assess your dominant conflict style.**

* Jeffrey H. Goldfien and Jennifer K. Robbennolt, "What If the Lawyers Have Their Way? An Empirical Assessment of Conflict Strategies and Attitudes toward Mediation Styles," *Ohio State Journal on Dispute Resolution* 22, no. 2 (2007): 277–319.

** "Conflict Management Styles Quiz," accessed Nov. 5, 2017; https://facultyombuds.ncsu.edu/files/2015/11/Conflict-management-styles-quiz.pdf. Based on Reginald Adkins PhD, "Elemental Truths."

Conflict Management Styles Quiz

Each statement below provides a strategy for dealing with a conflict. Rate each statement on a scale of 1 to 4 indicating how likely you are to use this strategy.

1 = Rarely

2 = Sometimes

3 = Often

4 = Always

Be sure to answer the questions indicating how you would behave rather than how you think you should behave.

1. I explore issues with others so as to find solutions that meet everyone's needs. _____ __

2. I try to negotiate and adopt a give-and-take approach to problem situations. _____

3. I try to meet the expectations of others. _____

4. I argue my case and insist on the merits of my point of view. _____

5. When there is a disagreement, I gather as much information as I can and keep the lines of communication open. _____

6. When I find myself in an argument, I usually say very little and try to leave as soon as possible. __ ___

7. I try to see conflicts from both sides. What do I need? What does the other person need? What are the issues involved? _____

8. I prefer to compromise when solving problems and just move on. _____

9. I find conflicts challenging and exhilarating; I enjoy the battle of wits that usually follows. _____

10. Being at odds with other people makes me feel uncomfortable and anxious. _____

11. I try to accommodate the wishes of my friends and family. _____

12. I can figure out what needs to be done, and I am usually right. _____

13. To break deadlocks, I would meet people halfway. _____

14. I may not get what I want, but it's a small price to pay for keeping the peace. _____

15. I avoid hard feelings by keeping my disagreements with others to myself. _____

Scoring

As stated, the fifteen statements correspond to the five conflict resolution styles. To find your preferred style, total the points in the respective categories. The one with the highest score indicates your most commonly used strategy. The one with the lowest score indicates your least preferred strategy. However, if you are a leader who must deal with conflict on a regular basis, you may find your style to be a blend of styles.

COLLABORATING

1: _____

5: _____

7: _____

Total _____

ACCOMMODATING

3: _____

11: _____

14: _____

Total _____

COMPETING

4: _____

9: _____

12: _____

Total _____

COMPROMISING

2: _____

8: _____

13: _____

Total _____

AVOIDING

6: _____

10: _____

15: _____

Total _____

Brief Descriptions of the Five Conflict Management Styles

Collaborating

Problems are solved in ways that provide an optimum result for all involved.

Both sides get what they want, and negative feelings are minimized.

Pros: Creates mutual trust, maintains positive relationships, builds commitments.

Cons: Time-consuming, energy-consuming.

Competing

Authoritarian approach.

Pros: Goal-oriented, quick.

Cons: May breed hostility.

Avoiding

The nonconfrontational approach.

Pros: Does not escalate conflict, postpones difficulty.

Cons: Unaddressed problems, unresolved problems.

Harmonizing

Giving in to maintain relationships.

Pros: Minimizes injury when we are outmatched, relationships are maintained.

Cons: Breeds resentment, exploits the weak.

Compromising

The middle-ground approach.

Pros: Useful in complex issues without simple solutions, all parties are equal in power.

Cons: No one is ever really satisfied, less than optimal solutions get implemented.

We've covered a lot of ground in Part I. With better understanding of how people make decisions, you have deeper insight into how decisions, personality, and conflict can affect the negotiation process. In Part II, we'll discover an effective strategy for negotiation—the Everybody WINS method.

Part II

The Everybody WINS Method of Negotiation

W: Wait
I: Identify
N: Negotiate
S: Settle on an Agreement

5

Wait

As we move into Part II, let's revisit our definition of negotiation.

---

*Negotiation is the process of creating an agreement
that is an acceptable outcome for everybody.*

Process: Negotiation is a process. This means that there are certain steps one must take to get from Point A (no agreed-upon acceptable outcome) to Point B (an agreed-upon acceptable outcome).

Creating an agreement: An important element of effective negotiation is creating agreement among the different parties. In order for the outcome to be truly an effect of negotiation, there must be some form of agreement.

An acceptable outcome: This is not the same thing as the best solution or ideal outcome. In negotiation, you must often trade something you want less for something you want more. But sometimes, what you want the most is to know that you've won. Again, we are defining negotiation as a *process*, which is different from an *outcome*. This book is designed to teach you a process that will increase the odds of a successful outcome.

For everybody: This is important. It's not negotiation if the outcome isn't truly an outcome that is acceptable to all parties. If one party feels cheated, coerced, or taken advantage of, it's not negotiation, it's manipulation.

To make it easy to remember, we've developed a four-step process for negotiation called Everybody WINS. WINS is an acronym that stands for these four steps in the process:

W: Wait. This means to wait until you've taken a look at your role in the negotiation and have explored the environmental factors that influence negotiations.

I: Identify. This means identifying the elements in the other party that are relevant to the negotiation.

N: Negotiate. This is the actual negotiation session or sessions. It's going back and forth with the other party until an acceptable outcome is established.

S: Settle on an agreement. This is coming up with the specific details of the agreement as negotiated between the parties.

The Scenario

In order to illustrate the Everybody WINS method, let's walk through a scenario that is very common in today's society—

the buying and selling of a home. This scenario will be carried through all of the chapters in Part II so that we can see the Everybody WINS process from beginning to end. Here are the details:

Peter and Penny are looking for a new home for their family. Their oldest daughter, Helena, has graduated from high school and is going off to college. They have one son living at home, Jack, who is severely disabled, and will not be able to live independently. They're ready to move to a more accessible home in an area that's closer to the services Jack requires.

Lee and Denise have been married a little more than a year now, and it's a second marriage for both. They each have two kids, although Lee's kids live with their mother, Linda. When Lee and Denise married, she moved into the home Lee had with Linda and brought her two sons, Chris and Eric. But despite her attempts to personalize the space and creatively redecorate the bedrooms, Denise can't help feeling as if she is living in another woman's home.

Lee, on the other hand, loves the house. He's been living there for ten years, and in that time has gotten everything just the way he wants it. From adding on a bonus man cave in the backyard, to putting in a pool, a waterfall, and a koi pond, Lee has invested a lot of time and money making the house into the perfect home for his personality. Plus, the property is near the ocean, and centrally located to the main area of town. Although he wants to make Denise and the boys happy, he's really reluctant to sell the house and start over again. But under pressure from his wife, he puts the house on the market, on a for-sale-by-owner basis.

It's been on the market a week or so when Lee gets an email from Peter and Penny, showing interest in the house. After two visits to the property, Peter and Penny are ready to make an offer.

For the purposes of illustration, we'll use the Everybody WINS process from the perspective of Lee.

Step One: Wait

Before you ever step into a negotiating room (literally or metaphorically), it's important to look at a few factors that will affect your negotiating strategy. If you don't do this, and instead jump in too quickly, you're likely to lose valuable negotiating power.

Here are some of the questions you want to answer:

1. Whom are you negotiating with?
2. What is your level of influence?
3. When is the best time to have this negotiation?
4. Where is the negotiation taking place?
5. Why do you want to win?
6. What is your desired outcome?

Let's take a look at these questions one at a time.

1. Whom are you negotiating with?

In some cases, this will be pretty obvious. If you're Madison in the opening scenario about eating chips before dinner, you're negotiating with your mother. If you're in an open vegetable market and are haggling with the vendor over the price of an item, you're negotiating with the seller.

But other times, it's not as clear. For example, when you go to purchase a car, it can appear that you are negotiating with the salesperson. But in reality the salesperson may be limited in what he or she can offer because of guidelines set forth by the sales manager or the manufacturer. As a general rule, you want to be sure to negotiate directly with the decision-maker. There's no point in hammering out an agreement only to find out later that the real decision-maker won't agree to it.

2. What is your level of influence?

As we learned earlier, influence is "the power to change or affect someone or something without directly forcing it to happen and without apparent effort." The amount of influence you have going into a situation can range from "no influence" to "some influence" to "high influence."

If you're trying to figure out where to go on vacation with your best friend, you've got high influence already. The other party values your opinion and cares about the relationship. If you're trying to get your airline seat upgraded by the ticket agent, you likely have no influence. The agent doesn't know who you are, and probably doesn't care where you sit on the plane.

Another way to look at the situation is through the dual-concern model: how much does the other party care about their relationship with you? Before you begin negotiation, it's important to get clear about how much influence you have on the person or people you're negotiating with.

3. When is the best time to have this negotiation?

This relates not only to the physical time, such as time of day or month, but also to the time in a given process. You're likely to have more bargaining power if you're negotiating a deal on a car in December because the dealership wants to liquidate its inventory before the calendar year changes. If you're buying a highly coveted item with limited supply right before Christmas, for example, you'll have less negotiation power.

Calendar time (time of day or month) can also affect the negotiation. Here are some issues relating to physical time that you want to consider.

Time of Day

The time of day when negotiations happen affects how alert and attentive people are and can affect your negotiations.

Early morning: Are you a morning person? Is the other party? If you're not at your intellectual best in the morning, then it's best to put off negotiations until you're at your peak. The same is true if the other person is also not a morning person, although it might be worthwhile to take advantage of that. Or you might wait until you have their clear attention. People are usually somewhat more alert after eating breakfast.

Late morning: By late morning, the day is usually in full swing, and most people are at their most productive. The other person may be feeling positive or may be distracted by the stressors of the day. But in general, this is an ideal time for negotiation.

Lunchtime: At lunch, people are more relaxed and may be more open to discussion and negotiation. A special consideration is the consumption of alcohol. Be very careful if you're drinking alcohol in a negotiation setting. While alcohol can smooth out tension and create a feeling of cooperation (and is often a culturally appropriate way to conduct business negotiations), be sure not to overindulge. Too much alcohol can affect your thinking.

Early afternoon: After lunch, we feel sleepy, as our digestive systems have more need for blood than our brains. You can use this to your advantage because the other party may be more likely to agree to your suggestions. But they may be distracted and not want to hear you out because they are feeling tired and still have a lot left to do in the day.

Late afternoon: This can be a good time to schedule negotiation, since people will often agree to your terms because they want to leave. It's not a good time, though, if you need to have the other party's full attention in order for them to understand what you're saying and agree to it. Their minds might be on the clock instead.

Dinner: Many of the factors that affect lunch are also present during dinner negotiations but intensified. People tend to be more relaxed and open. It can be a good time for more subtle persuasion techniques rather than hardline negotiation. With a full stomach, a relaxed environment, and maybe even a glass of wine, the other person may be more amenable to suggestions that they would have rejected outright earlier in the day.

EVENING: We don't often think of evening as a time for negotiation. If you're negotiating at night, outside the workplace, be sensitive to the fact that the other party may have defenses up that might not exist during the daytime. Think of the salesperson in your home after work in the evening versus one coming over in the late morning.

Day of the Week

The day of the week affects negotiation as well. Of course, you can't always control the day of the week that you're negotiating, but if you can choose, consider these factors.

MONDAY: There's a reason Monday has a bad reputation. People are often not happy to be back at work, they may be tired from the weekend, or they may be overloaded with a new workweek. Before you negotiate with someone on a Monday, check their mood. If the other person isn't in an ideal state for negotiation, then either flex your style to accommodate this or see if you can choose another day.

TUESDAY: Tuesday—especially Tuesday morning—is an ideal time to negotiate. The other party is over the Monday blues, and yet it's not so close to the weekend that they are distracted by that.

MIDWEEK: Wednesday and Thursday are also solid choices, although the later you go in the week, the more stress and fatigue the other person may be feeling. If the other person has goals to reach by the end of the week, then depending on how they are doing, they may be either relaxed or anxious and focused.

FRIDAY: TGIF can be a negotiating tool. People are usually very productive on Friday morning, as they want to get everything done before the weekend. If you want the other person to be decisive, this is a good time to negotiate. The environmental load is usually pretty high, and the other person isn't likely to want a lot of information or take a lot of time to hear what you have to say. If, however, you want the person to carefully consider your ideas, choose early Friday afternoon. This will give the person the weekend to think about what you've proposed. Late Friday can go either way. The person may already be on the weekend mentally, and so may not want to hear what you are proposing, or they might concede to your wishes just to get you out the door.

THE WEEKEND: During the weekend, people are often at their most relaxed. Thoughts relating to home, family, and leisure take over from work issues, usually. If the subject of negotiation is personal, a weekend meeting might be effective. There is also the possibility, though, that the other person may have limited time and attention, because social and family obligations may be taking their attention. Usually the weekend isn't a good time to talk about work-related issues, unless the other party is a workaholic type A who never stops thinking about work, or if you're actually at work on the weekend.

*   *   *

Generally, when the other party is engaged in an activity that takes their attention away from you, whether it's because of the time of day, the day of the week, or the setting, you'll want to consider that when negotiating. Timing can work to your advantage if you want them distracted and not focused. Or it can be a disadvantage if you need their full attention and focus. If they are likely to fight you or present conflict, choose a time when they are more relaxed than not.

Remember what we learned about stress and negotiation. The other person may be triggered into fight or flight. If possible, avoid the fight. If they are inclined to flight, then they may be more likely to satisfice, and to seek any solution to reduce the stress. You can use that to your advantage and get them to make concessions to you.

Finally, take a look at how near the negotiation is to an event, if relevant. As we learned, when environmental load increases, stress increases. People tend to become more decisive or get stuck in analysis paralysis.

4. Where is the negotiation taking place?

Negotiations take place in many different formats. Is yours taking place in person? By phone? Over the internet? In writing? Your physical proximity to the other person sets a tone of intimacy or distance.

If you have a breakfast meeting, for example, it's a more casual environment, and the act of eating and drinking is more communal. Plus the caffeine and food will wake you up.

If you buy lunch for the other party, you can trigger feelings of reciprocity, which can cause them to concede more to you during the negotiation.

If possible, try to have the negotiation on your home turf. Second best is to have the negotiation in a neutral environment. But if the person has more power than you, and you need to be on their turf, be aware that it can influence the dynamic. We'll get more into that in a later chapter of the book.

5. Why do you want to win?

After looking at the external factors, such as time and place, and before walking into the negotiation, it's important to do some soul searching. To paraphrase a famous song. . . . "you don't always get exactly what you want, but you might get something you need." Ask yourself, "Why do I want to win?" Sometimes the answer is straightforward: "I want to win so that I can get a raise and earn more money for my family." But sometimes the answer is less tangible. It may have to do with pride, competition, or ego.

That's not to say that these are bad reasons to want to win. But you have to be aware of a tendency toward something called *escalation of commitment* or winning at all costs. We'll get into that in greater detail in the next chapter, as it is something you can use to your advantage.

6. What is your desired outcome?

This is perhaps the most important question to ask before you begin negotiating. What do you want? If you're not clear about the specific outcome you want, you're not likely to get an ideal outcome.

There are two basic kinds of outcomes to any negotiation: quantitative, or those you can measure, and qualitative, those you cannot. Quantitative outcomes are items such as money, time, or physical objects. Qualitative outcomes are things that aren't tangible, such as maintaining the relationship with the other person, or increased feelings of happiness, trust, respect, self-esteem, or some other internal state. In the potato-chip scenario, the outcome that Madison most wanted was a feeling of winning rather than the actual chips.

When figuring out what you want, identify your ideal outcome. Be specific because it will give you information for negotiation. Make a list of what you want from the situation, and then give a weight to how important each of those things are to you.

Putting It All Together

Let's look at Lee, our home seller, and apply the Wait factor to his situation.

1. Whom are you negotiating with?

In this case, Lee is negotiating with two parties, his wife, Denise, and the potential buyers, Peter and Penny. The dual-concern model applies here, because he wants to make his wife happy, but he also wants to negotiate the best deal with Peter and Penny.

2. What is your level of influence?

Because he is married to Denise, Lee has a fairly high level of influence over her. He has a moderate influence over Peter and Penny, because he has only met them during the home visits.

3. When is the best time to have this negotiation?

For Lee, the best time to negotiate would be a time when Peter and Penny are somewhat distracted. From the home visits, it was clear to Lee that they really loved the house. Peter in particular was taken by the man cave. Penny liked the proximity to town. Helena, the college-bound daughter, loved the pool. So, because Lee is in the power position, dealing with an interested buyer on his home turf, he wants to take advantage of that in the negotiation.

4. Where is the negotiation taking place?

Ideally from Lee's point of view, the negotiation would take place at the house, so that Peter's and Penny's emotion about wanting the house and envisioning living there would give Lee the strategic advantage.

5. Why do you want to win?

For Lee, there are two motivations. One, he wants to get the most return from his financial investment in the house. Two, he wants to feel that, even though he has had to sell his precious home, at least he got a good price for it. The first is quantitative, and the second is qualitative.

6. What is your desired outcome?

Lee made a list of his ideal outcomes and weighted his criteria on a scale from 1 to 10. It looks like this:

What I Want in This Situation

Item	Weight
To not have to sell the house	10
Enough money to buy a bigger house for Denise and all four kids (at least $650,000)	9
For Denise to be happy with the outcome	10
For all four kids to be happy with the outcome	9
A ninety-day escrow	7
The buyers to pay for any needed repairs or replacements	7
An all-cash deal	8
Buyers who appreciate the house and its quality	8
Buyers who will live in the house and not flip it	8

In this chapter, we've looked at the W in the Everybody WINS process of negotiation. In the next chapter, we'll take a look at identifying the factors that involve the other party.

6

Identify

In this chapter, we'll look at the second step in the Everybody WINS process. Remember, the four steps are as follows:

W: Wait. This means to wait until you've taken a look at your role in the negotiation and have explored the environmental factors that influence negotiations.

I: Identify. This means identifying the elements in the other party that are relevant to the negotiation.

N: Negotiate. This is the actual negotiation session or sessions. It's going back and forth with the other party until an acceptable outcome is established.

S: Settle on an agreement. This is coming up with the specific details of the agreement as negotiated between the parties.

*   *   *

After you've considered what you want, as well as the environmental factors, such as time and place, then it's time to look at the other party. Clearly identifying what they want (as best you can tell) will help you to understand their bargaining position, and what you can offer that will appeal to their wants.

Specifically, you'll want to look at the following questions.

1. What does the other party want?
2. What are each party's interests and agendas?
3. Why do they want it?
4. What are the barriers to cooperation?
5. What is negotiable?
6. What are some alternatives that might satisfy agendas and interests?

Let's look at each of these questions in greater depth.

1. What does the other party want?
As we have learned, most people have more than one concern in a negotiation. They want a certain outcome, but they also often have another competing concern, often a relationship of some sort. This becomes an internal conflict between the people and the problem.

For example, when Dad comes home from work and notes, "This place is a mess!" he may be simply identifying a problem. But the family may hear it as a personal attack. Mom thinks, "Hey, I work all day too. Why is it my responsibility to clean the house alone?" The kids may think, "There goes Dad again, always complaining about something." In other words, there are usually two issues at hand—the people and the problem. In order to effectively negotiate with other people, we have to overcome our almost automatic tendency to blend the two.

One way to do this is to list your assumptions about what the other person wants and why. In the case of Lee, it might look like this.

Denise wants a different house because:

- She is jealous of Linda and the life I had with her.
- She hates making love in the bedroom where I was with Linda.
- She doesn't like the style of this house.
- She wants a bigger house with more bedrooms and bathrooms.
- She wants a house without a pool.
- She thinks this house is too expensive to keep up and wants a less expensive home.
- She thinks I spend too much time in my man cave.
- She wants to be in a better part of town.
- She thinks that I want to get back together with Linda.

Next Lee separates out the people issues from the problem by questioning those assumptions. Are they valid? In order to actually determine their validity, he might have to ask Denise. This isn't always feasible when both the relationship and the negotiation are contentious. In that case, one must simply be aware of the assumptions, and separate out the people issues from the problem issues. After talking with his wife, Lee discovers the following.

What Denise actually wants from the sale of the house:

Valid assumptions:
- She wants a bigger house with more bedrooms and bathrooms.
- She thinks this house is too expensive to keep up and wants a less expensive home.

Flawed assumptions:
- She wants a house without a pool.
- She wants to be in a better part of town.

Note that these are the issues that relate to the actual substance of the problem, not the ones that relate to Denise.

Always separate the issues with people from the issue of the problem.

Even if you don't like the other party, you can have an effective negotiation with them. Here is one way to look at it: Let's say that you and the other party are sitting at a table, opposite each other. In the middle of the table is a piece of paper that represents the issue or problem at hand. Typically each of us sits there and tries to get as much of the paper over to our side of the table as possible. In the Everybody WINS method, you both come around to the same side of the table and focus on the piece of paper, instead of trying to get it to your own side.

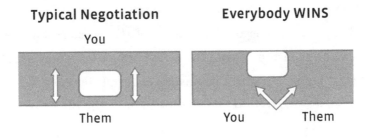

By focusing on the problem at hand, you're better able to craft an outcome that meets your needs and addresses the other person's needs as well.

In Lee's case, the issue at hand is the house, why Linda wants to sell it, and what the asking price will be. This is different from everyone's feelings about the house.

2. What are each party's interests and agendas?

This is not to say that the other person's psychological factors are not relevant. They are. In their landmark book *Getting to Yes*, Roger Fisher and William Ury say it this way:*

> Understanding the other side's thinking is not simply a useful activity that will help you solve your problem. Their thinking is the problem. Whether you are making a deal or settling a dispute, differences are defined by the difference between your thinking and theirs. When two people quarrel, they usually quarrel over an object—both may claim a watch—or over an event—each may contend that the other was at fault in causing

---

* Roger Fisher and William Ury, *Getting to Yes: Negotiating Agreement without Giving In* (New York: Penguin, 1991).

an automobile accident. The same goes for nations. Morocco and Algeria quarrel over a section of the Western Sahara; India and Pakistan quarrel over each other's development of nuclear bombs. In such circumstances people tend to assume that what they need to know more about is the object or the event. They study the watch or they measure the skid marks at the scene of the accident. They study the Western Sahara or the detailed history of nuclear weapons development in India and Pakistan. Ultimately, however, conflict lies not in objective reality, but in people's heads. Truth is simply one more argument—perhaps a good one, perhaps not—for dealing with the difference. The difference itself exists because it exists in their thinking. Fears, even if ill-founded, are real fears and need to be dealt with. Hopes, even if unrealistic, may cause a war. Facts, even if established, may do nothing to solve the problem.

So it's critical to identify the way the other party is thinking about the issue. Going back to Lee and Denise, here are the items that relate to her thinking.

Denise wants a different house because:

• She is jealous of Linda and the life I had with her.
• She hates making love in the bedroom where I was with Linda.
• She doesn't like the style of this house.
• She thinks I spend too much time in my man cave.
• She thinks that I want to get back together with Linda.

Regardless of whether or not these things are actually true, if Denise actually feels this way, then it becomes a factor in the negotiation. Fortunately, Lee can actually talk to Denise and clarify those assumptions.

As mentioned, however, it's not always feasible to talk to the other party. Lee doesn't know Peter and Penny well enough to be able to ask them their thoughts about buying a house.

There are almost as many interests and agendas as there are people in a negotiation. Here are some examples.

- Wanting to look good to another person
- Wanting the satisfaction of winning
- Avoiding loss
- Affirming one's self-concept
- The norm of reciprocity ("If I do this, then she will do that.")
- Revenge
- Taking care of one's children, or extended family
- Getting in or out of a situation ("I just want it to be over." versus "I'll do anything to get in the club.")
- Saving face or avoiding embarrassment

3. Why do they want it?

In 1943, psychologist Abraham Maslow developed a theory about human needs as motivators for behavior. It's commonly called Maslow's hierarchy of needs, and the idea is that as humans we have core needs that need to be met before we can care about higher-order needs.* This diagram represents the levels of needs.

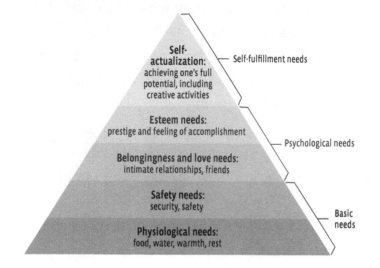

Later in his life, Maslow extended and modified the model, but the central idea is useful here. When looking at the other party's interest in a negotiation, it's important to understand that offering a higher-order item such as including the patio furniture in a home sale is not going to be appealing when one's lower-order need such as enough money for the down-payment hasn't been met. If the other party in the negotiation doesn't have enough money to buy food, they're not going to value a lifetime-achievement award.

Furthermore, you can be in more than one level. After all, the human mind is complicated and has many different thought processes running at the same time.

So looking at what Penny and Peter want in buying his home, Lee might observe the following:

---

* Abraham Maslow, *Motivation and Personality* (New York: Harper, 1954).

Since they have a disabled son, Jack, they are likely to be concerned with his safety. So the pool might be an issue. But they also want to be close to town so that they can be near their son's doctors. It's a beautiful home, by the beach, so they might have a sense of pride and accomplishment in being able to live in such a prestigious neighborhood, while at the same time taking care of their son. The man cave might be a good place for Peter to get some space, and the koi pond could be a tranquil place for Penny to sketch or paint.

4. What are the barriers to cooperation?

Before you ever walk into the negotiation, it's important to identify any barriers to cooperation that might be present— why the other party might not want to cooperate with you. The reasons can be many, but here are some common barriers to cooperation.

1. **YOU**: You might not want to think so, but you might be a primary barrier to cooperation. How have you behaved toward the other party in the past? What is your attitude now? Are you coming into the negotiation with a hostile or negative mindset? Review chapter 5 and check to make sure that you're not unintentionally creating a barrier to cooperation.

2. **THEIR RELATIONSHIP WITH YOU**: Clearly a person who has had a contentious relationship with you in the past isn't likely to suddenly become cooperative. In situations such as divorce, hostile takeovers, and disagreements between neighbors or family members, your relationship with the other party

might make it so that they aren't very willing to work with you collaboratively. That's why it's so important to separate the people from the problem.

3. POWER: Power differentials can play a huge factor in whether or not the other person is willing to negotiate with you. If they have more power than you do (a boss, a parent, someone with more money or status), and they perceive the negotiation as a win-lose, they are not likely to want to cooperate.

4. THE STATUS QUO: If the other party doesn't see the status quo as being particularly bad, they won't be too inclined to change it. They may very well just dig in and become stubborn. After all, why should they agree to a change?

5. THEIR INTERESTS AND AGENDAS: As mentioned previously, the other party may have some irrational reason that they don't want to cooperate with you. As we talked about in chapter 1, people will avoid making a decision because they fail to identify a serious risk if nothing is done—in this case, to cooperate with you.

5. What is negotiable?

Another area to identify before you go into the negotiation is exactly what elements are negotiable. These include items such as terms, pricing, timing, options, flexibility, or more.

In Lee's case, his thoughts might go like this:

With Peter and Penny, the things that are negotiable are the selling price, the down payment, length of escrow, seller financing, whether I leave the furniture and the koi, inspection, and who pays for closing costs.

With Denise, the things that are negotiable are when we sell the house (now, or in a year or two), where we move after the house is sold, and, in fact, whether we should sell at all rather than keeping the house as a rental property.

When you are getting ready to enter negotiations, try and think of as many points of compromise as you can. This way you can craft an offer giving up items that don't matter so much to you in favor of the things you really want. "I'll leave the furniture and the koi if they put up a full 20 percent of the selling price as a down payment."

6. What alternatives might satisfy some agendas and interests?

It's a good idea to brainstorm some alternatives that satisfy the nontangible agendas and interests. For Lee, putting Denise on the title of the house might be an alternative that would keep her from feeling that she's living in another woman's home.

- Ideal outcome
- Worst outcome
- Most likely outcome

For Lee it might look like this (we will discuss the BATNA/WATNA model in chapter 9):

BATNA: Best alternative to a negotiated agreement

My best alternative would be keeping the house and having Denise be happy with that choice. Short of that, my best alternative would be to get the full asking price of $650,000, or above, with an all-cash buyer, have a longer escrow, and not have to pay closing costs.

WATNA: Worst alternative to a negotiated agreement

The worst outcome would be that we sell the house and lose money on it, and Denise is still not happy. My kids are mad at me, and I can't afford to buy another home that is as nice as the one we sold. This means that I can't accept a price less than $610,000.

MLATNA: Most likely alternative to a negotiated agreement

The most likely alternative is that the buyers will offer $625,000. I'll come back with a counter of $635,000 and they'll accept. Denise will be happy; my kids will not.

In this chapter we've identified the issues that relate to the other party in the negotiation. Now it's finally time to negotiate.

In other words, what is the best outcome you would accept? What is the worst outcome that could happen? And what's the most likely outcome?

7

Negotiate

As expected, Lee and Denise receive an offer on the house. But they are stunned to find that it is a full 10 percent below asking price. Because they are selling their home themselves, they don't have a real estate agent to offer advice. The house has been on the market for five weeks for sale by owner, and this is their first offer.

"I think we should take it," Denise says.

"Ten percent below asking price is ridiculous. It's almost offensive, really. My preference would be to just say no and wait for another buyer," Lee says.

"Why? I think we were overpriced, actually, and that's why we haven't had any other offers. I think we should counter, but keep it within their ballpark. What if we counter and they walk away? Besides, there is something about this couple I like. I think they would really appreciate the house."

Lee isn't sure what to do. He didn't want to sell the house in the first place, but is doing so only to make his wife happy.

Now he's feeling pressured to accept a price that is far lower than he feels is fair.

After sleeping on it, he decides that although he is confident that there will be another buyer if this one backs out, his wife is not, and, frankly, her feelings are more important than getting top dollar. So he invites Peter and Penny over to talk about it.

Up until now, this part of the book has focused on the events that happen before the negotiation begins. This chapter and the next will cover the actual process of negotiation.

As we mentioned previously, negotiation can take place in many forms. It can be as casual as a conversation between two friends deciding where to go for dinner ("Let's go for Italian food tonight and then Chinese food next time."). Or it can take place in a formal setting like a courtroom ("Will the plaintiff be satisfied if the defendant pays for half of the damages caused by the tree?").

Regardless of the formality or complexity of the negotiation, there are some commonalities. When you are negotiating, consider these three areas:

1. The **process of negotiation**. This is how we are negotiating.
2. The **substance**. This is what we are negotiating about.
3. The **relationships**. This, of course, relates to how the relationship affects the negotiation, and how the negotiation affects the relationship with the other party.

In the case of Lee, he is concerned about his relationship with Denise. That concern affects both how he negotiates with her and how he negotiates with Peter and Penny. If Lee were to do or say something that would have a negative effect on Denise, his relationship with her would suffer.

Too often, we get into a negotiating situation and forget about the long-term impact on relationships. While negotiating, and this book, are about winning, the concept of winning encompasses preserving and maintaining positive relationships—a concept that is so important that it bears repeating.

Negotiation is not a game where you try to win, make the other party lose, or carry out a personal vendetta or grudge.

Let's continue with our story, as Penny and Peter arrive to make their offer.

"Thanks for meeting with us like this, Lee," Peter says as he takes a seat next to his wife in the living room they hope will be their own soon. "We really love your home and are hoping we can come to some kind of a deal."

Denise replies, "We do too. You seem like a great family. Jack is lucky to have you."

"Well, that's the thing," Penny replies. "It's been rather expensive having a permanently disabled child. And now with Helena going off to college, we don't really have a lot of money. We need to move closer to the hospital, as the severity and frequency of his seizures are increasing. Frankly, there's

not a lot else out there on the market. We have some constraints but would love to buy your house."

Pausing to think for a moment, Lee realizes that he just
discovered a few important things in the negotiation so far.
Peter and Penny love the house. Few other houses on the market are available to satisfy their needs. They have an urgent
reason to be near the hospital. And they have money challenges. Lee is also picking up on Denise's eagerness to sell the
house to this family, both because she is eager to close the
deal and because she likes the people. He can use this information in the negotiating process so that he can come up with
options that benefit everyone.

Mutual-Gains Negotiation

As we have noted, our definition of negotiation involves a
process that is intended to result in an outcome that is agreeable to everybody. This means developing options for mutual
gain rather than figuring out a way to get the most from the
other party.

A type of negotiating called *mutual-gains negotiation* is
designed for just that.*

> The Mutual Gains Approach (MGA) to negotiation is a process
> model, based on experimental findings and hundreds of real-
> world cases, that lays out four steps for negotiating better out-
> comes while protecting relationships and reputation. A central
> tenet of the model, and the robust theory that underlies it, is

---

* Susskind, Lawrence, and Patrick Field. *Dealing with an angry public: The mutual gains approach to resolving disputes.* Simon and Schuster, 1996.

that a vast majority of negotiations in the real world involve parties who have more than one goal or concern in mind and more than one issue that can be addressed in the agreement they reach. The model allows parties to improve their chances of creating an agreement superior to existing alternatives.

This, of course, fits with our dual-concern model, and it's what Lee is facing. Here are the four steps of the mutual-gains approach.

1. Preparation
2. Value creation
3. Value distribution
4. Follow-through

Since we have covered preparation in a previous chapter and will cover value distribution and follow-through in a later chapter, we'll focus on value creation here.

Value Creation

Value creation involves inventing without committing. In other words, when the other party shares (or you discover) an interest, then both parties declare a period of inventing without committing, during which they advance options by asking, "What if?" By brainstorming different solutions, options, and outcomes, both parties can discover ideas they might not have thought of before. Again, it's about both parties coming around to the same side of the table and working together to solve the problem.

In Lee's case, some of the ideas that come out of value creation might sound like this:

"Okay, I am hearing that we each have some different considerations here. My wife really likes your family and wants to sell to you. But I have a price factor, in that I put a lot of money and sweat equity into this place and want to see a return on it. If I'm being honest, I don't really want to sell at all.

"You guys seem to like the house, but price is a factor for you as well. *What if* we spent the next ten minutes or so brainstorming different options that would create mutual gain? But no one is committing to any of the options at this point; we're just putting ideas out there. Is that okay?"

After getting agreement on that, the two couples spend the next few minutes coming up with creative ideas.

"What if we agreed to a price that's higher than our offer, but with less money down?"

"What if you did a lease with option to purchase, where you put little money down, and have the option to buy when Helena graduates from college?"

"What if you agreed to full asking price and then sold the koi? There are easily fifty koi in the pond, and they are high-quality fish, so they are probably worth at least $100 each, if not more. If you wanted to, you could even sell the filters and other equipment for another $10,000."

Engaging with this process gets the parties thinking about different options and what is important to them. How much do Peter and Penny want koi? Are they insistent on buying a house now, or would a lease option work for them?

In the inventing without committing process, parties can discover additional interests, create options that had not previously been imagined, and generate opportunities for joint gain by trading across issues they value differently.

Interests versus Positions

Let's look a little more deeply at the idea of interests versus positions. The Everybody WINS process is designed to keep you focused on interests rather than on defending a position.

Interests: This is what you or the other party say you want.
Positions: This is the underlying reason why you want it.

Often people take positions because they believe the position addresses their interests. But as we are seeing, rarely is that position the *only* way to address interests. Sometimes the other party's position conflicts with your interest. That's why the Everybody WINS process is about discovering a position that can address both parties' interests. Here are some examples.

Interest: I would like to get a raise.
Position: They aren't paying me what I'm worth.
Possible option: Nonfinancial rewards, such as time off.

Interest: I need money to get my car repaired after the accident.
Position: Those people are going to pay for what they did to my car!
Possible option: The other party completes the repairs themselves.

Interest: I want to keep the house in the divorce.
Position: She cheated on me, and now I want her to suffer the consequences.
Possible option: She buys out my equity in the house over time.

In the case of Lee, here is how the mutual-gains approach and value-creation exercise helped clarify interests and positions and develop options that satisfy all.

Interest: Peter and Penny want the house for significantly less than asking price.
Position: With a disabled child and a daughter in college, they can't afford to pay full price for the house.
Option: Agree to paying a higher price than the offer and put less money down.
Option: Agree to paying full asking price and then sell the koi in the pond and the equipment.

Interest: Lee doesn't want to sell his house at all.
Position: He loves that house and put a lot of time and effort into it. He has an emotional attachment to the house.
Option: Peter and Penny lease the house with the option to buy when they have more money after Helena graduates from college.

Interest: Denise wants to sell the house and move into a different one.
Position: She doesn't want to be living in the shadow of Lee's first wife and their life together in that house.
Option: Any of the solutions presented here will satisfy her interests.

Separating Positions from Interests

Despite your best efforts in preparation, it's not always easy to separate out people's positions from their interests. To that end, University of Washington professor Vandra L. Huber identified these twenty-two questions you can ask and statements you can make to separate positions from interests:*

1. Correct me if I am wrong . . . but what if we?
2. We appreciate what you've done/are trying to do.
3. Our concern is fairness.
4. We would like to settle on the basis of principle, not on the basis of selfish interest or power.
5. Trust is a separate issue.
6. Could I ask you a few questions to determine if my facts are correct?
7. What's the principle behind your action/proposal?
8. Let me see if I understand what you're saying . . .
9. Let me get back to you on that by _____
10. Let me explain why I have trouble following some of your reasoning . . .
11. Is a trial basis/period possible?
12. If we disagree, the implications are . . .
13. What are you trying achieve by . . . ?
14. Could you reword your proposal?
15. Could you explain what we both can gain by your proposal?
16. Let me see if I understand your concern . . .
17. Would you consider . . . ?

---

* Vandra L. Huber, "Twenty-Two Questions to Help Separate Positions from Interests," accessed Nov. 6, 2017; http://faculty.washington.edu/vandra/html/neg22quests.html.

18. Could you explain what problems you see with my proposal?
19. How can we decide what is reasonable or what is fair?
20. Can we break the issue into more manageable parts?
21. I understand that's your position, but could you explain what it is you are concerned about?
22. Why do you think that proposal/price is reasonable?

When you are negotiating, it's important to stay focused on generating solutions that satisfy the parties' interests while taking their positions into account. We'll get more into how to avoid making mistakes, as well as some tips and techniques in later chapters.

For now, let's move on to the next chapter and discover how to craft an agreement.

8

Settle On An Agreement

"Can I refill your coffee?" Denise asks, walking into the living room with a freshly brewed pot.

"Actually, we just got a text message from Jack's caregiver saying she needs to leave early. Would you mind if we ran home to get him? We'd only be gone an hour."

"Oh, of course! No problem. I'll keep your coffee warm."

Just as Peter and Penny drive away to get Jack, Lee notices an alert on his phone. "Denise, you are not going to believe this. Somebody else just put in an offer!"

"What? Who?" Denise is shocked—and thrilled! "How much?"

"Full price! All cash!" Both Lee and Denise were stunned. But they also wonder, "What's the catch?"

They do a little research on the potential buyer and discover that it is a real estate investment group that has been buying up properties in the neighborhood with the intent of turning the block into a strip mall.

"Wait, aren't those the people who strong-armed Mr. and Mrs. Wilson until they finally sold?" Denise asks.

"Yeah, they are. They want to buy our house, because the Nelsons on the other end of the block refused to budge."

"But they'd tear it down and put up a strip mall! Honey, I'd hate to see that happen to the house you love so much," Denise says.

Lee is feeling dejected and torn. On the one hand, he could accept a full-price, all-cash offer and walk away with all of his financial goals from the transaction met. And his wife would be happy to see the house sold.

On the other hand, not only is Lee selling his house, but it's to an impersonal investment group that is literally going to tear it down. He isn't sure he could bear that.

In this chapter, we'll cover the last letter in the acronym WINS: *settle on an agreement.*

This scenario shows exactly why the Everybody WINS process makes sure to identify what you really want. What is most important to you? What is less important? Let's go back to chapter 5 (see page 58), and the exercise Lee did that clarified what he wants.

In this case, it's prudent for Lee to pull out this exercise and revisit his weights. After meeting Penny and Peter and receiving an all-cash offer from buyers who intend to raze the property, how does he feel? Are the weights the same? He looks at each one, and considers revising it.

What I Want in This Situation

Item	Weight	Weight Adjusted
To not have to sell the house	10	10
Enough money to buy a bigger house for Denise and all four kids (at least $650,000)	9	9
For Denise to be happy with the outcome	10	10
For all four kids to be happy with the outcome	9	9
A ninety-day escrow	7	7
The buyers to pay for any needed repairs or replacements	7	6
An all-cash deal	8	6
Buyers who appreciate the house and its quality	8	9
Buyers who will live in the house and not flip it	8	9

Thinking about it, Lee realizes that some of the weights stay the same. He still really doesn't want to sell. But if he has to sell, he wants to make sure he gets enough money out of it that he can afford another, equivalent home. He wants his wife and kids to be happy. He realizes, though, that he's not as concerned with the buyers paying for repairs as he thought he was. And an all-cash deal isn't as important to him as it is selling the house to the right buyer, who will live in and appreciate the house that he so lovingly created.

There are times when what we want in a negotiation changes. This can happen as a result of things that are said and done in the negotiation, or from changed external circumstances.

Before agreeing to an outcome, it's always a good idea to revisit your original list and make sure that your priorities haven't changed.

Before agreeing to an outcome, it's always a good idea to revisit your original list and make sure that your priorities haven't changed.

Value Distribution

As we continue to explore the mutual-gains approach, it's time to look at *value distribution*. Value distribution is a way of determining who contributed what to the final agreement. The best way to do this is to establish objective criteria that everyone can use to justify their "fair share" the value they each contributed to the agreement.

Therefore, to get the other party to agree to your solution, you need to present your proposal in such a way that the other party can see that it's in their best interest to accept it.

An important way to do this is anchoring.

Anchoring

Anchoring is a term that describes the phenomenon that occurs when the first proposal in a negotiation is set forth. Whoever makes the first proposal is establishing an "anchor" or a base from which the rest of the negotiation follows. Should you make the first move? Should you wait for the other party to do so? There have been many different theories about this.

Law professor Charles B. Craver writes:*

Some individuals commence bargaining encounters with modest proposals hoping to generate reciprocal behavior by their opponents that will generate pleasant and cooperative win-win interactions.

Opening offers that are overly generous to adversaries are likely to have the opposite effect due to the impact of anchoring. When people receive more generous offers than they anticipated, they question their own preliminary assessments and increase their own aspirations.

They begin to think that they will be able to obtain more beneficial results than they initially thought possible, and they move psychologically away from the other side. They thus make opening offers that are more favorable to their own side.

It is important for parties commencing bargaining encounters to plan opening offers that favor their own side, but which can be logically explained to provide them with credibility.

In my Legal Negotiating class, students get identical fact patterns pertaining to a tort claim. The students are told that they all represent the defendant, and they are asked two questions. What is the first offer you plan to make in response to the plaintiff's initial demand? And how much do you think you will finally have to pay to resolve this claim?

* Charles B. Craver, "The Impact of Psychological Factors on Bargaining Negotiations," Alternatives to the High Cost of Litigation website, June 11, 2011; http://www.altnewsletter.com/sample-articles/psychological-factors-bargaining-interactions.aspx.

Half of the students are told the plaintiff has demanded $100,000, and half are told the plaintiff has demanded $50,000. The half facing the initial $100,000 demand plan higher opening offers and think they will have to pay more to resolve the claim than the students facing the $50,000 demand.

GAIN/LOSS FRAMING

Individuals can significantly enhance the probability of opponent acceptance by the manner in which they frame their offers.

People tend to be risk averse when they must choose between a sure gain and the possibility of a greater gain or no gain. But they tend to be risk takers when they have to choose between a sure loss and the possibility of a greater loss, or no loss.

I demonstrate this to students and to attorney-practitioners in my Legal Negotiation courses by asking the following questions:

1. Assume you must choose between the following two options:
   - If you select Option 1, you receive $100.
   - If you select Option 2, there is a 20% probability you will receive $500 and an 80% probability you will receive nothing.

Most individuals prefer the certain $100 gain over the risk of no gain associated with Option 2.

2. Assume you must choose between the following two options:

- If you select Option 1, you have to pay $100.
- If you select Option 2, there is a 20 percent probability you must pay $500 and an 80 percent probability you have to pay nothing.

Most persons select Option 2 in this scenario. They are unwilling to accept the sure loss, and prefer the alternative that may enable them to avoid any loss—despite the fact this choice may cause them to lose more. . . .

Negotiators who are formulating offers should strive to frame their offers as sure gains—instead of sure losses—to their opponents. In almost all business dealings, whether one is the buyer or seller, or the licensor or the licensee, negotiators can articulate offers that appear to be gains to the offer recipients. This factor increases the likelihood their offers will appeal to the other parties.

Gain/loss framing is especially relevant with respect to lawsuit settlement discussions. Defendants almost always appear to be offering sure gains to plaintiffs—and their attorneys, who are usually compensated on a contingent fee basis—causing both plaintiffs and their counsel to be hesitant to decline certain gains in favor of possibly greater gains or no gains.

On the other hand, plaintiffs appear to be demanding what seem to be sure losses from the perspective of defendants, causing them to be more risk taking in an effort to avoid the certain losses.

How can plaintiffs try to reverse this impact? If they frame their offers by suggesting that for $XX, the defendant's problems will be resolved, they may be able to make their demands seem like "gains" to the defendants.

Framing the Offer

As we've discovered, how we frame the initial offer has a large impact on how the other party will receive it. This is why it was so important to complete the I (in WIN) step in the process before ever beginning the negotiations. The more you know about the other party, their interests and positions, and how they think and reason, the better you are able to match your solution to their gains.

Let's go back to Lee and Denise, and the dilemma they're in with the two offers. First, Lee must negotiate with Denise so that they can come to an agreement on which offer to take.

"Denise," Lee asks her, "before Peter and Penny get back, we should decide what we are going to do about the other offer. What are your thoughts?"

"Well, as much as you don't want to sell the house, I know you do want to get as much money for it as you can. Financially, it seems like we should take the highest offer. But I'm not sure. After everything that happened with the Wilsons, I don't like the idea of the house being turned into a Mini-Mart. And I really do like Peter and Penny. I know they would love the house."

"What if we came up with a solution that meets everyone's needs?" Lee suggests. "Except those of the investment group, of course. I think I like the idea of the lease option. Peter and Penny live here and lease the property for four years, while their daughter is in school. Then, at the end of that, they have the option to buy it."

"How would we come up with the money to buy another place?" she asks.

"What if, before they moved in, we sold the koi and the pond equipment? I put a ton of money into that stuff, and the koi have been breeding like crazy. I'm sure I could get $15,000 at least for it. We could take that, and the money we got from Aunt Jacquie's inheritance as a down payment for another place."

"So we move, like I want," says Denise, "we don't sell the house right away, like you want, and Peter and Penny can live in a house that they can't really afford at the moment. I like it! Tell the investors to take their offer and . . . well, you know."

Smiling at his wife, he put his arm around her and said, "Well, let's just wait until we have a firm deal with Peter and Penny first."

Lee was able to use value distribution to help Denise see that the solution he proposed is the ideal outcome for everyone. Now it's time for him to frame the offer with Peter and Penny. First, he is going to tell them about the other offer, to create a sense of urgency and scarcity. He's also wisely waiting to decline the other offer, in the chance that Peter and Penny say no.

"Thanks for waiting," Peter says, as Penny wheels Jack in the front door. "Claire doesn't usually need to leave early, but her mom needed the car for something. This is Jack."

"Nice to meet you!" Lee and Denise are struck at the sight of a seventeen-year-old who is the size of an elementary schooler, with crazy blond hair and a twinkle in his eyes that make him look like an old man.

"Another thing we like about this place is how accessible it is. No stairs."

Directing them into the living room, Lee gets down to business. "So, while you were gone, Denise and I were notified that we have another offer on the place. It's a full-price, all-cash offer."

Peter and Penny look visibly shaken as they glance at each other. "Oh. Well, there's no way we are going to be able to match that." They start to stand up again, and say, "Thank you for your time, anyway—"

Denise then interjects, "The thing is, we really like your family. Even more now that we've met Jack. We want you to have the house but want to find an arrangement that works for all of us."

Curious, Peter and Penny sit back down. "What do you have in mind?"

Lee then explains his proposal, framing it so that Peter and Penny see the gains and no losses.

"If you lease for four years while Helena is in college, you'll be able to save up more for a down payment, and you'll be able to live in a house that is accessible, near to Jack's doctors, and is, as you've said, better than any of the options you've seen."

Peter is still unsure, as he is focusing on potential losses. "Yes, but if we lease versus buy now, we'll still be throwing away thousands of dollars on rent instead of building equity in a place of our own."

"What if we did this?" Lee proposes. "Let's set a specific purchase price that you'd have the option of taking in four years. We'll set a rent that is slightly above our current mortgage, and we put the difference in an account. At the end of the four years, we'll use that amount as a credit toward your down payment toward buying the house. If you don't buy the house, though, the money goes to us."

Peter and Penny looked at each other thoughtfully. "Can we take a walk and talk about it? This is really different than what we were thinking originally."

"Of course!" Denise smiled. "I'll just stay here with Jack and get to know him better."

A few minutes later, Peter and Penny come back in, smiling. "We have a deal!"

After handshakes between the men, and hugs between the women, Lee says, "Okay, let's hash out the specifics of the lease amount, the purchase price, and all relevant dates. Then I'll get my sister, the attorney, to write up the contract, and we'll courier it over to your place tomorrow."

In the scenario, after negotiating with Denise, Lee then framed the offer with Peter and Penny so that they could see his solution as one that provides them with maximum gains and minimal losses. When they countered with an objection, he modified the offer to accommodate it. When negotiating an offer, it's important to pay attention to these considerations:

- Get everyone committed to a mutually beneficial outcome.
- Specify all points of agreement.
- Make sure that they are objectively quantifiable.
- Put it in writing!

After the Negotiation

Once the agreement has been reached and put in writing, the Everybody WINS process is not quite done. You have to follow through.

This means you need to look ahead to identify anything that might derail the agreement in the future and build in contingencies for the things that might go wrong.

Everybody WINS

Although our scenario with Lee and Denise is straightforward, and there wasn't much hostility between the parties or conflict, it is a good illustration of the steps in the Everybody WINS method of negotiation.

W = Wait
 I = Identify
N = Negotiate
S = Settle on an Agreement

Using the Everybody WINS model in negotiation can result in an outcome that is beneficial to all parties—even if it's an outcome that neither party had thought of originally.

In Part III of this book, we'll look at some of the real-world applications and challenges of Everybody WINS.

Part Three

Everybody WINS
in Action: Real-World
Applications

9

Common Mistakes

Last year Bill authorized a $500,000 expenditure for a transition of his company's technology to a cloud-based platform. Unfortunately, the company they chose to help with the transition, SimTex, has proven to be less than ideal. They seem to be juggling too many projects, and Bill is constantly being told there are delays, glitches, and problems with the migration.

The SimTex people tell him that with an infusion of another $35,000, they will be able to complete the transition, and Bill should start seeing returns on the investment within a year.

But how is Bill going to convince management to invest another $35,000 into a project that's already cost half a million dollars, and isn't even complete? Should he negotiate with SimTex so that they absorb the additional costs? Should he just spend the extra money and risk further losses, or cut off the project and accept the half-million-dollar write-off? Bill truly doesn't know what to do.

In the example we used in Part II, the negotiation between Lee and Denise and Peter and Penny was cooperative. This was so that we could illustrate the Everybody WINS method more easily. But clearly, in the real world we often find ourselves negotiating with other people who don't care to be using the Everybody WINS method. What do you do then?

This chapter covers some of the mistakes that people tend to make when negotiating with others.

Not Developing a Plan B

No negotiation technique is fail-proof. Sometimes, despite our best efforts, we are unable to come to an agreement with the other party. In *Getting to Yes*, Roger Fisher and William Ury write that you should think about your alternatives to negotiation in three ways:

BATNA: Best alternative to a negotiated agreement
WATNA: Worst alternative to a negotiated agreement
MLATNA: Most likely alternative to a negotiated agreement

In other words, if you're not able to come to an agreement, what are your alternatives? What is the best alternative? The worst? The most likely?

Let's say you are flying to Italy to attend your sister's wedding when you're informed that you've been bumped off the flight in New York. Despite your best attempts to negotiate, it's clear that you are not going to be on the plane.

BATNA: The best alternative is that you get on another flight within the hour and still make it to the airport in Rome at roughly the same time as planned.

WATNA: The worse alternative would be for you to not get on another flight until tomorrow, and you miss the wedding.

MLATNA: Most likely, you'll have to wait a few hours and will get on another flight and should still be able to make the wedding.

The BATNA approach is an effective tool in negotiation because it can be used to generate alternatives in negotiation. Fisher and Ury offer three suggestions for accomplishing this:

1. Inventing a list of actions one might take if no agreement is reached
2. Converting some of the more promising ideas and transforming them into tangible and partial alternatives
3. Selecting the alternative that sounds best

In the case of the airplane flight, you might ask the reservation agent to look at other airlines with flights to Italy, or to route you through another city to get to Italy.

We'll get more into the BATNA model and how to use it in a later chapter.

Escalation of Commitment

In 1976, researcher Barry Staw presented his study in a paper titled "Knee-Deep in the Big Muddy: A Study of Escalating

Commitment to a Chosen Course of Action."* In it he established a concept called *escalation of commitment*, which went on to spark a lot of research. It's also been called the *sunk-cost fallacy*. The basic idea is that there is a human tendency to continue with a committed course of action, despite negative consequences, because we are focused on how much we've already invested in that course of action.

Staw demonstrated this in groups with the Vietnam Dollar Exercise. It was so called because it was developed during the Vietnam War to illustrate how the US government kept sending troops to Vietnam, despite mounting evidence of negative consequences. Here's the exercise.

In front of a group, you hold up a dollar bill, and say, "I will auction off this dollar. I'll start the bidding at five cents, and if you are the second highest bidder, you have to give me the money, even though you won't get the dollar. So if you bid ten cents, and someone else bids fifteen cents, you still have to give me the ten cents."

The first person bids 5 cents, hoping that no one else will bid and that he will make a 95-cent profit. The second person bids 10 cents, and now the 5-cent bidder has to choose to bid 15 cents, or lose his 5 cents. This goes on, with each bid getting successively larger. An interesting thing happens when one of the bidders goes to a dollar. Now the second highest bidder, who bid, say 85 cents, either has to bid $1.05 to win the dollar (thereby really only losing 5 cents), or lose 85 cents. The game shifts from maximizing the win to minimizing the loss.

---

* Barry M. Staw, "Knee-Deep in the Big Muddy: A Study of Escalating Commitment to a Chosen Course of Action." *Organizational Behavior and Human Performance* 16.1 (1976): 27–44.

What happens, almost inevitably, is that the two bidders keep going and going, attempting to minimize their losses, until they are paying far more for a single dollar than the value of the dollar.

In fact, when business professor Larry Pate (one of Staw's original students), conducts this exercise in class, he observes this phenomenon to an exaggerated degree. He says, "I once had two students who each didn't want to 'lose' to the other, such that they were no longer bidding for the value of the dollar, but to 'win.' Eventually, they each bid more than $14 for the dollar. That's what happened in Vietnam."

When you are negotiating, it's important to be aware of a human tendency to escalate commitments. When you defend your position, you become more and more committed to it. Of course, you can also use escalation of commitment to your advantage, but be careful not to lose your rationality so that you end up betting more than what the item you're bargaining for is worth.

The more you clarify your position and defend it against attack, the more committed you become to it.
—William Ury

Getting Past No

In *Getting Past No* (the sequel to the popular *Getting to Yes*), William Ury identifies several obstacles to cooperative negotiation, and the things you should avoid doing.* These are the five obstacles:

1. **Your reaction**. Your emotional reaction to the thoughts, feelings, and actions expressed by the other side.

2. **Their emotion**. The emotional disposition of the other side, which can be driven by fear, anger, or zero-sum thinking.

3. **Their position**. The other side's expression of and insistence upon what they want to get from the negotiation (not why they want it).

4. **Their dissatisfaction**. The other side's view of your options for agreement, which may cause them to lose face.

5. **Their power**. The other side's perspective on the power they possess in the negotiation, which may affect their willingness to act cooperatively.

To counter these obstacles, and break through to cooperation, Ury offers five "don'ts" along with five "dos." Here are the "don'ts":
• Don't react.
• Don't argue.
• Don't reject.
• Don't push.
• Don't escalate.

---

* William Ury, *Getting Past No: Negotiating with Difficult People* (New York: Bantam, 1991).

Here are the corresponding "dos":

· Do go to the balcony.

· Do step to their side.

· Do reframe.

· Do build them a golden bridge.

· Do use power to educate.

Let's go through them one at a time.

Don't React: Do Go to the Balcony

When you feel yourself starting to react emotionally to what the other person is saying or doing, mentally step outside the situation and view the negotiation from a higher perspective. This allows you to distance yourself from your emotions and avoid striking back or getting involved in escalation of commitment. As Ury puts it, it takes two people to entangle the negotiation into an unproductive conversation, but it only takes one person to prevent it.

To "go to the balcony," take a break. Step outside. Get a drink of water, go to the bathroom. Find some way to physically leave the space, if possible, so that you can remind yourself of the objective outcome you are trying to accomplish.

Don't Argue: Do Step to Their Side

This is the same thing as our "come around to the same side of the table" concept from before. Here's what Ury suggests doing in order to achieve that.

· Listen carefully to the other party's perspective and then repeat what they said, using your own words: "I hear that you feel it's unfair for you to have to pay more than 50 percent of the expenses." This is not the same thing as agreeing, by the way. It's simply acknowledging that you've heard what they said.

- Use the word *yes* a lot and get them to say it too. This stimulates the part of the brain that is associated with cooperation and sets a cooperative tone for the conversation.
- Similarly, don't use the word *but*, as it negates everything that comes before it: "We agree that the fence is too high, but it blocks our view." Instead, say "Yes, and . . .": "Yes, the fence is high, and it still blocks our view."
- Use an optimistic tone and body language. Lean forward, openly, and make eye contact. Don't lean back with your arms crossed. Don't use a harsh tone of voice or overly direct language, but instead one that is softer.

Don't Reject: Do Reframe

Instead of rejecting the other party's statements, reframe them from positions to interest. Since you have already investigated their interests in the I phase of the Everybody WINS process, you should be able to do this easily: "Look, we all want the same thing—for the kids to be happy." If you don't know the other party's interest, here are some ways to determine it.

- Ask the other side open-ended questions, such as "why" or "why not?" This will cause them to explain themselves in a way that reveals their underlying mindset.
- Ask for their "advice" on what they would do if they were you. "If Bill, on the other side of your house, put up a large

fence that made it so that you couldn't see the view we all pay for, what would you do?" Then, follow up with "why" or "why not?"

- Don't be afraid of silence. Too many of us are uncomfortable with silence and fill it with chatter. Silence can be your ally in negotiation. When you ask a question, make an offer, or present an option, then be quiet. Chances are, the other party will get uncomfortable enough to answer first.

- No matter what they say, or how hostile they get, reinterpret what they say into something positive. "You're just too lazy to get a job, and so you want me to pay more child support" becomes "We both want the children to have what they need, we just differ on what that is."

Don't Push: Do Build Them a Golden Bridge

The fourth "don't" is not to pressure the other side but help them come to see your solution as the optimal one. We talked about this earlier in terms of framing. Here are some of the obstacles you may need to overcome.

1. The other party may reject the idea because it wasn't theirs.

2. The other party may have interests that haven't been met yet.

3. The other party may lose face or experience some form of embarrassment or reputation damage as a result of accepting your proposal.

4. The other party may feel pressured or rushed to agreement.

Remembering back to the section about the different conflict styles, you can use that information to reframe the objections. Here are some other suggestions, based on *Getting Past No*.

- To prevent them from rejecting an offer because it wasn't their idea, get them involved in forming it. This can happen during the value-creation process, where each side is brainstorming ideas together.
- Ury says that the basic human being needs areas for recognition, identity, and security. Present your ideas in such a way that the other party sees that they meet these core needs.
- If the issue is one of losing face, continue to work to find a solution that prevents that. "What if someone else was the one to actually tell the employees?" Or, if they are resistant to *any* solution you propose, have a neutral third party present it.
- Help the other side to see your options or proposal as being a win for them, and they are more likely to accept it.
- If the other party is feeling rushed or pressured, back off. As we learned in the decision-making section, feeling time constraint can lead to either satisficing or overanalysis. One way to deescalate the pressure is to assure the other party that considering an option or proposal is not the same thing as accepting it, and accepting a proposal is not usually a permanent decision. Reassure them that no commitment will be made until *all* parties are satisfied with the outcome.

Don't Escalate: Do Use Power to Educate

This last "don't" is a warning not to strong-arm or coerce the other side. Instead, help them to see that what you are proposing is the BATNA (best alternative to a negotiated agreement). Here are some suggestions.

- Use facts and questions to highlight the negative consequences of not agreeing. "Given that the courts usually side with the mother in cases like this, it seems like this is a good solution."

- Remind the other party that the proposed settlement is in both of your best interest, you're not trying to "win" or take advantage of them; you're just trying to solve a problem.

Here are some additional dos and don'ts that are based on ideas from Charles B. Craver, in his article "Classic Negotiating Techniques."*

Don't casually dismiss an extreme initial demand or offer.

> People confronted by extreme opening positions should not casually dismiss them, because this approach may lead opponents to believe their wholly one-sided demands or offers are more realistic than they initially thought. Recipients of such offers should politely but firmly indicate that they are completely unreasonable and unworthy of serious discussion. Such communications can induce the original offerors to moderate both their internal objectives and their external position statements in the other side's direction.
>
> An effective way to counteract extreme opening positions involves the use of probing questions. Offerees can ask offerors a series of questions requiring those persons to explain the

---

* Charles B. Craver, "Classic Negotiation Techniques." *Negotiator*, Feb. 2007; http://negotiator magazine.com/article356_1.html.

rationales supporting each aspect of their opening positions. The questioners should begin with the most finite components where there is little room for extreme puffing and then move on to the less finite aspects. If the unreasonable offerors are forced to explain each component, they begin to falter since it is difficult to defend wholly realistic positions with respect to such finite items as lost wages or the value of real estate.

If you're the one making an extreme opening offer, be prepared to logically explain each component and match them to the interests of the other party.

Watch out for the "nibble technique."
This is when the other side agrees to "final" terms, only to come back later with some "slight changes." What happens is that you get into an escalation of commitment and are more likely to agree to the changes, because you have already committed to the agreement.

Since their unsuspecting opponents are psychologically committed to final agreements and do not wish to allow these modifications to negate their prior efforts, they give in to the requested changes. This allows the nibblers to obtain post-agreement concessions that are not reciprocated by themselves.

Individuals confronted by nibbler opponents need to be "provocable" if they wish to avoid exploitation. When their opponents inform them of the necessity for modifications, they should demand reciprocity. They should indicate that their clients have some qualms of their own and suggest that they can accommodate the changes being requested if their concerns can be simultaneously satisfied.

If the persons demanding post-agreement changes are actually sincere and their clients really have to have several changes, they will recognize the principle of reciprocity and make concessions in exchange for the modifications they are seeking. If they are disingenuously employing the nibble technique to extract unreciprocated, post-agreement concessions and they are confronted with demands for reciprocity, they will most likely realize that they are better off accepting the original terms agreed upon. They will withdraw their demands for post-agreement modifications.

Don't react to strategic anger.
This is when the other party becomes angry in an attempt to intimidate you into either giving up your position or agreeing to theirs.

When opponents seem to become angry, most persons respond in kind. This often causes problems as the battle escalates. The best way to respond to strategic "anger" is the opposite of what is expected. If opponents stand over someone and shout, those victims should remain calm and silent. They should listen carefully for verbal leaks that may inadvertently disclose important information. They should also look at their opponents as if they are acting like children. It is difficult to have a one-way harangue for long without becoming embarrassed. As the demonstrative parties feel ashamed of their behavior, they tend to make concessions in an effort to regain social acceptability.

Similarly, if the other party hangs up the phone, ends a video conference, or walks out in anger, let them go.

Use the Br'er Rabbit technique with highly competitive opponents. This is when you strategically frame your real objective as a win for the other party.

> Joel Chandler Harris created the unforgettable character named Br'er Rabbit. When he was caught by the fox, he asked to be skinned or to have his eyeballs ripped out, as long as he was not flung in the briar patch. The fox tossed him in the briar patch and he escaped. This technique is based on reverse psychology. People employing this technique indicate a preference for Items 1 and 2, but suggest a willingness to accept Item 3 if they can't have what they prefer to obtain. Item 3 is their real objective.
>
> This tactic can be especially effective against highly competitive win-lose opponents who are only satisfied when they think their counterparts have completely lost. They thus try to give others what they think those persons least wish to obtain. If the Br'er Rabbit approach is used effectively against them, they will force the other side to accept Item 3 instead of the other two things that side professes to want, causing their counterparts to leave with exactly what they wanted.

Don't argue with the "bad cop."
In some negotiations, you have two people on the opposing side; one will be tough and the other will appear more accom-

modating. Craver calls this the "Mutt and Jeff routine." The natural tendency is to argue with the tough one, but instead you should focus on the more cooperative one.

The Mutt and Jeff routine is one of the most common—and often effective—negotiation tactics. One seemingly reasonable negotiator softens opponent resistance by thanking them for their kind treatment and requesting seemingly modest proposals. Opponents are pleased to give them what they are seeking. As soon as they do, however, the unreasonable partners of these persons completely trash these concessions and demand substantial changes. When the opponents are about to explode, the "good cops" calm their "bad cop" partners and request additional concessions. When they obtain better terms, the bad cops attack the new offers being made. As obvious as this Mutt and Jeff technique can be, it is amazing how often negotiators succumb to these tactics. They work so hard to please the bad cops that they fail to appreciate how effectively they have been fleeced.

Most people confronted with Mutt and Jeff opponents make the mistake of arguing entirely with the bad cops. What they should do is focus on the good cops. When these seemingly reasonable persons indicate they would accept the terms if a couple of modest changes were made, they should be directly asked if they would agree if these modifications were made. They should be forced to say "yes" or "no." Once it becomes clear that they will not say "yes" without the concurrence of their bad cop partners, the game is over and they have to change tactics.

Don't fall for the country bumpkin routine.
This is when the opposing party acts like a simpleton who can't understand complex topics. "I'm just a good ole boy from the South. We just keep things simple down there." Craver likens this routine to the detective character of Columbo, played by Peter Falk.

> Some sly negotiators emulate the Lt. Columbo character created by Peter Falk and act like bumbling idiots. They say that they don't know anything about these types of interactions and indicate a willingness to allow their "fair and knowledgeable" opponents to determine what would be appropriate for both sides. They hope to lull unsuspecting opponents into careless disclosures and concessions intended to help these seemingly inept bargainers. In the end, these Br'er Rabbit negotiators leave with everything, and their opponents are so glad they could help solve their problems. These are highly manipulative negotiators. Individuals should never feel sorry for seemingly incompetent adversaries. They should ignore such behavior and execute their planned negotiation strategy. If such opponents seem willing to give in to their demands, they should take advantage of their willingness to be exploited. Once those people realize that their technique is not working, they will end their charade and act more normally.

In this chapter, we covered some of the ways you can avoid making mistakes when negotiating. In the next chapter, we'll talk about what to do if the other party doesn't want to play fair.

10
What-Ifs

Ted can't believe she did it again. Despite the court order that established his visitation every other weekend, when he goes to pick up his daughters, Lindsey and Jamie, from their mother's house, no one is home. Angrily, he dials his ex-wife's cell phone number.

"Patsy. Where are the girls?"

"They're with me. Why?"

"Because it's Friday. I'm sitting outside your house in my car, trying to pick my daughters up for my weekend with them, and they're not even here."

"Oh, yeah. Well, they needed haircuts."

"You know you're not supposed to make plans or appointments during my visit times. We've been through this a million times. You have them all week, and every other weekend! Get their nails painted or whatever then!"

"Sorry, Ted. You know how teenagers are. Just come back tomorrow morning, and they'll be ready."

After hearing the line disconnect, Ted sits there staring out the window, trying to decide what to do. Patsy has a habit of doing this—completely violating the custody arrangement. And if Ted tries to say anything about it, she bad-mouths him to the girls and threatens to move out of state in order to be closer to her mother. Ted doesn't want to risk further damaging his relationship with his daughters, but it's not right that Patsy should be allowed to totally violate their agreement like this. He just doesn't know how to handle it.

In an ideal world, all negotiations would go smoothly and result in a satisfactory outcome, and both parties would be fair and honest. Unfortunately, that's the stuff of Disney movies. While many negotiations do go smoothly (especially if the parties use the Everybody WINS method), the sad reality is that not everyone plays fair.

This chapter will cover several scenarios where the other party is less than cooperative, despite your best effort.

What If the Other Guys Play Dirty?

Vandra L. Huber identified several "dirty tricks" that people tend to use in negotiation, as well as what you can do to counter them.*

1. Phony Facts

Typically, the numbers appear valid but the assumptions upon which the numbers or conclusions are based are dubious.

---

* Vandra L. Huber, "Dirty Tricks and What You Can Do about Them," accessed Nov. 7, 2017; http://faculty.washington.edu/vandra/html/body_negdirty.html.

Example: "You need to buy an Airbus plane. We have far fewer plane crashes and accidents than Boeing does."

Counter Tactic: Ask them to state their assumptions or explain how they derived their numbers.

2. Higher Authority

It is common for a negotiator to delay reaching an agreement by claiming that his or her authority is limited. The other party will become impatient and give in to the earlier demands. Alternatively, it gives the negotiator an out if the settlement is not desirable.

Example: "Well, your proposal sounds interesting, but I will have to take it back to my boss for final approval."

Counter Tactic: Find out who the person with authority is and negotiate with that person initially. Appeal to the person's ego and say, "So you don't have any authority. I thought you were the decision-maker."

3. Add-ons

A common tactic used in sales negotiations. Negotiator asks for a small concession and adds it on to the item already being negotiated.

Example: "I'll take the computer if you will throw in free maintenance for a year."

Counter Tactic: Recognize the tactic for what it is. Give them the add on if you would have anyway. If not, say no.

4. Personal Attacks

A variety of tactics fall under the heading of personal attacks. They are all designed to make you feel uncomfortable and to make you forget about your real negotiation objectives.

Example: They can attack your status, ignore you during a negotiation, fail to make eye contact, or comment negatively on your appearance, your intelligence, or integrity.

Counter Tactic: Call it for what it is. Refocus the negotiation on the problem at hand.

5. Good Guy/Bad Guy

One person plays the good guy; the other, the bad guy. Good guy tries to keep negotiation moving in desired direction. Bad guy imposes limits.

Example: "Joe is really tough to deal with in these situations. Maybe if you can give in a little, I can talk some sense into him."

Counter Tactic: Identify the tactic and discuss it openly.

6. Intimidation

A variety of influence tactics fall into this category including anger, fear, emotional ploys and guilt. They may also claim there are legitimate channels to go through.

Example: "How dare you make such a low offer. You must know nothing about the airline industry."

Counter Tactic: Go to your balcony when you feel your emotions taking over for your reason. When you are calmer, collect information to counter the intimidation.

7. Lock-in Tactics

Communication strategies which force the other party to make concessions.

Example: A foreign national publicly announces that it will not withdraw its troops. Because the statement is public, the other side gives in.

Counter Tactic: Recognize the ploy for what it is and publicly acknowledge it as a tactic. Proactively, state that such tactics will not be tolerated.

8. Take It or Leave It

This is really not a negotiation approach. It is, however, an approach to conducting business which blocks negotiating.

Example: "This is the salary we are offering for the position. If it is unacceptable, then we will have to select someone else for the position."

Counter Tactic: Call their bluff. Ignore and keep on talking.

9. High Ball/Low Ball

Negotiator starts with an extremely high or low opening offer. As we have noted, this affects the decision anchor point, and adjustment from the opening offer is usually insufficient. Risk is that other party may consider negotiation is a waste of time.

Example: "We will offer you $100,000 for the house (when it is worth $250,000)."

Counter Tactic: Identify in advance your BATNA. Have objective information to counter their offer. Ask them to justify the offer.

10. Bogey

Negotiator pretends an important issue is not important. Later in the negotiation, the item of value can be traded. Useful if you can identify an issue that IS important to the other side but of little value to your side.

Example: "Our budget only allows us to pay so much."

Counter Tactic: Never accept the assumption on face value. Find out why the budget is fixed.

11. Chicken

Negotiator combines a bluff with a purported action. It is a high risk strategy. If the other side calls their bluff, they must be willing to carry through with the action.

Example: "If you don't accept our offer, we will close the plant."

Counter Tactic: Ignore the bluff and keep on talking or call their bluff.

12. Exaggerated Assertions

Negotiators may intentionally describe interests, time preference or needs one way when they want them to go another way.

Example: "I've really got to have that item delivered by Friday."

Counter Tactic: Call them on it. Give them what they want if it is of low value to you and then leverage that to help get what you want.

13. Threats

A tactic used if one party has the power to inflict relatively large punishment on the other without substantial retaliation.

Example: "If that assignment is not completed by Friday, I will fire you."

Counter Tactic: Determine if the threat is valid, if they will actually follow through on it, and if it's a false threat, call their bluff. If it's a valid one, suggest that you will go over their heads and say that you were threatened.

14. Scoundrel

An unethical maneuver. The scoundrel lures an opponent into a deal by making an attractive offer. Once the other person is mentally committed, the scoundrel reneges on the deal and uses a variety of tactics to repudiate the deal (higher authority, legal delays, lost paperwork).

Example: "Yes, we did have a deal but that was before I knew you needed A and B and C. Those, of course, will be additional costs."

Counter Tactic: Run, don't walk away at the first indication that you are dealing with a scoundrel. If it is too late, get the best legal help possible.

15. Scrambled Eggs

The negotiator deliberately makes a deal complex to create confusion.

Example: Car leasing agreements have come under attack recently for being so complex that individuals do not understand what they are really paying for the leased car.

Counter Tactic: Admit the negotiation is becoming too complex and go to your balcony until you have time to analyze the situation.

16. Foot in the door

The negotiator gets you to make a small concession. He or she then builds from that base to get you to make more concessions.

Example: "If the price is right, will you buy a car from me today?"

Counter Tactics: Know what your negotiation latitude is in advance and stay within that range.

17. Deadlines

Imposing a time limit often sets the boundaries on a negotiation. Too often people accept another's time deadline as their own.

Example: "I need to have your decision on this matter by Friday at 5 p.m."

Counter tactic: Determine why this deadline is important. Explain and impose your own deadline.

What If They Won't Negotiate with Me at All?

In their book, *Everyday Negotiation*, authors Deborah Kolb and Judith Williams state that there are actually two "conversations" that happen in any negotiation. First is the overt subject of the negotiation—the topic at hand. The second is what they call the *shadow negotiation*. It is here, Kolb and Williams assert, that "the parties decide between them whose interest and needs command attention, whose opinions matter, and how cooperative they are going to be in reaching an agreement."*

In other words, underneath every negotiation is a power play, if you will, between the people doing the negotiation. In the case of Lee, Denise, Peter, and Penny, the shadow negotiation was played out on equal footing. But, in the case of Ted and Patsy, it is not.

The Everybody WINS method of negotiation can actually help elucidate the issues in the shadow negotiation.

Let's look at an example. Cathy has just interviewed for a job at a prestigious accounting firm. For her to take the job, she'll need to move from Texas to California, and because the living expenses are going to be higher, she'll need a salary that is significantly larger than what she has gotten in her previous positions. She mentioned this in the interview, and the interviewer nodded, made a note of it, and moved on with the interview.

When Marcy calls her to offer the position, she mentions that the salary is about 10 percent below what Cathy needs

---

* Deborah M. Kolb PhD and Judith Williams PhD, *Everyday Negotiation: Navigating the Hidden Agendas in Bargaining* (San Francisco: Jossey-Bass, 2003): 12.

to make ends meet. Cathy doesn't want to risk having Marcy rescind the job offer, but she also needs to make sure that she can afford to live at the same standard of living as she does now. So she attempts to negotiate the salary.

"Marcy, I am really excited to join your team and get started. The thing is, we're a little way off on the salary."

"What do you mean?"

"In the interview, I mentioned that I need at least $72,000 base salary to afford to live in California. Your offer of $68,000 is quite a bit off from that."

"Yes, I remember that. But you'll also note that we've built in a generous bonus and benefits package that adds to the overall compensation."

"I appreciate that, but I'm afraid I can't count on an end-of-year bonus to cover my monthly expenses."

"Well, the best I can do is to possibly get you an extra week of vacation time per year. But we really don't have the budget to flex on the salary. We do have a fair number of others who interviewed for this position, and none of them indicated a problem with the salary. I'm afraid that the salary is firm."

Now what should Cathy do? When she went through the W stage of Everybody WINS, she identified what she needs to get out of the negotiation. She is very clear that she needs a specific salary in order to take the job. But it appears that Marcy won't negotiate.

Again, using Everybody WINS, Cathy would have already answered the questions about what Marcy and the company want.

1. **What does the other party want?** Marcy wants to hire a great accountant to join the firm.

2. **What are the other party's interests and agendas?** Marcy's interest is in filling the position at the salary and benefit level offered. Her agenda, or position, is that the job is a coveted one and she doesn't need to budge on salary.

3. **Why do they want it?** Marcy wants to hire someone to distribute the workload better. She also needs to hire someone, because three people left the company in the last year.

4. **What are the barriers to cooperation?** The primary barrier to cooperation is a power differential. Marcy has a job open, and Cathy wants it. Marcy doesn't need to cooperate with Cathy.

5. **What is negotiable?** It appears that the base salary isn't negotiable, but a bonus package, vacation, and other benefits are negotiable.

6. **What are some alternatives that might satisfy agendas and interests?** To have leverage with Marcy to entice her to negotiate, Cathy needs to even the power dynamic. To do this, she needs to demonstrate that she is a better choice than the other candidates, and that she is worth the effort for Marcy to work cooperatively with Cathy to find a way for her to take the job.

Let's continue on with the conversation between Cathy and Marcy.

"I hear what you're saying: that the base salary isn't flexible," says Cathy. "I understand your dilemma. Let me reiterate, though, that with fifteen years' experience, and multiple certifications, I'll be able to bring in business to justify the higher salary within the first quarter. I also know that you've had a fair amount of turnover this year. Is it possible that there are some funds for a signing bonus that would come out of the end-of-the-year bonus? Also, if the company paid for my moving expenses, that would free up my budget so that I could accept the lower salary for a few months. What if the offer was at the base salary you suggested, but with a signing bonus, moving expenses, and an agreement that we will revisit my salary in six months to determine if I've brought in enough new clients to justify a raise?"

If Marcy still refuses to budge, then Cathy has a strong preview of what it will be like to work there. Sometimes the best negotiation tactic is to value yourself enough to walk away.

Sometimes the best negotiation tactic is to value yourself enough to walk away.

What If You Have No Negotiating Power?

The scenario that we've just seen with Cathy is an example of what can happen when there is a power differential between the two parties in negotiation. There are a few factors at play when you are negotiating with someone with whom you have little or no negotiating power.

First, you need to do a reality check. Many times we assume we have no power in a situation when we really do.

Writer Carolyn O'Hara, in an article in the *Harvard Business Review*, points out, "Having power typically reduces a person's ability to understand how others think, see, and feel, so being in the less powerful position actually gives you a better vantage to accurately assess what the other party wants and how you can best deliver it. And when you do your homework, you'll often find you've 'underestimated your own power, and overestimated theirs,'" adds management consultant Jeff Weiss, as quoted by O'Hara.*

O'Hara goes on to say, "Do some hard investigation of whether those concerns are real and consider what skills and expertise you bring to the table that other candidates do not. The other side is negotiating with you for a reason." As Margaret Neale, a professor of management at the Stanford Graduate School of Business, says, "Your power and influence come from the unique properties you bring to the equation."

This leads to the second aspect—evening out the power differential. Very often, as was the case with Cathy, it comes from knowing your own value and worth in the situation. It's as much an attitude and a demeanor as it is about facts.

In addition, evening out the power differential involves asking questions (like the ones in chapter 7) so that you can put the other party in a position of defending and explaining their position.

---

* Carolyn O'Hara, "How to Negotiate with Someone More Powerful than You," *Harvard Business Review*, June 6, 2014; https://hbr.org/2014/06/how-to-negotiate-with-someone-more-powerful -than-you.

Weiss goes on to say, "Two of the most powerful strategies you can deploy are to listen well, which builds trust, and pose questions that encourage the other party to defend their positions. If they can't defend it, you've shifted the power a bit." If your boss says he doesn't think you are the right addition to a new project, for instance, ask, "What would that person look like?"

O'Hara offers these points to remember:

Do
- Put yourself in their shoes—it's crucial to understand what's important to the other side.
- Remember your own value—you are at the table for a reason.
- Ask questions—you'll get valuable insight into their motivations and interests.

Don't
- Wing it—nothing beats good preparation.
- Depend on a single strategy—develop a range of responses to push the negotiation in your favor.
- Copy aggressive behavior—if they make threats or demands, stick to your goals (just avoid reacting emotionally).

It's also important to have developed your BATNA—your best alternative to a negotiated agreement. That is, what will you do if you can't reach an agreement? This will help remind you that it's not necessarily the end of the world if the negotiations fall through. You have a Plan B.

What If the Other Party Doesn't Uphold the Agreement?

As we saw in the scenario with Ted and Patsy and the visitation with their daughters after the divorce, even when you have a negotiated agreement, sometimes the other party doesn't uphold it. In this case, you have two options. Sometimes you can take legal action (with a court order or legally binding agreement). But that is often expensive and time-consuming.

Alternatively, you can revisit your BATNA. What is your best alternative to the negotiated agreement? After all, short of legal or other intervention, you can't *force* another person to uphold an agreement.

In the case of Ted and Patsy, his thoughts might go like this:

"Okay, my BATNA is that I just see the girls when I can, and do my best to create a warm loving relationship with them that will outlast this temporary problem with their mother. My end goal in visitation is to be close to my kids, and fighting with Patsy isn't really the best way to do that.

"My WATNA is that she moves away and takes the girls. If she does that, I'll talk to them, and see if they want me to go for custody. At a minimum, I'll get a revised court order for visitation.

"The MLATNA is that Patsy will continue to break the agreement whenever she wants, and I'll just have to deal with it. The key here is not to engage with her, and hopefully she'll stop fighting me."

Chapter 10 covered some of the what-ifs in negotiation. Next, let's look at how differences between people play out in negotiation.

11

Individual Differences In Negotiating

"Terry, are you there? I have a question to ask you," Antonio says in an instant message to his colleague early one morning.

"I'm here. What's up?"

"I want to ask Mark for a raise. It's been eighteen months since I started working here, and they said that my salary was a starting salary. What do you think I should do?"

Antonio and Terry work for a company that has employees all around the world. With teams in Latin America, North America, Eastern Europe, and Asia, cultural differences often come into play. The owner of the company, Mark, is from the United States, as is Terry. Antonio is from South America.

"Absolutely, Antonio. You should ask for a raise. You have nothing to lose."

"Do you think I should call him? Email? Text?"

"Write him an email. That way he'll have time to read it and think it over."

Antonio sends over the following draft:

"Dear Mark, I would like to talk with you about raising my salary, if possible, at a time that is convenient for you. If you do not want to discuss it at this time, that is fine, too. Please let me know. Antonio."

Terry writes back, "Antonio, would you mind if I take a pass at this? I can see some areas for improvement." Her draft looks like this:

"Mark, it's been a year and a half since I started working here, and I really love the job. I am writing to request a raise in my salary, as we discussed when I was hired. Specifically, I'd like an extra $500 per month, beginning next month. I believe I can justify the raise, because I have brought in several new clients this year, and go above and beyond the call of duty, working weekends and nights when necessary. I'm happy to discuss this by phone if you wish. Thank you in advance. Antonio."

Antonio is thrilled. "Terry, I like your draft much better. Can you tell me why, please, is my draft not so good?"

Antonio is seeing the impact of cultural differences in communication and negotiation. Mark, as an American, is a very direct communicator. He's going to want the email to get straight to the point, be as specific as possible, and use facts to support his request. Antonio, from South America, is more indirect and polite, as well as informal. If he had sent the email he wrote, his chances of getting the raise would have been greatly diminished.

In an article in *Ivey Business Journal*, author Jeswald W. Salacuse highlights these top ten ways that cultural differences can affect negotiation:*

1. Negotiating goal: contract or relationship?
2. Negotiating attitude: win-lose or win-win?
3. Personal style: informal or formal?
4. Communication style: direct or indirect?
5. Sensitivity to time: high or low?
6. Emotionalism: high or low?
7. Form of agreement: general or specific?
8. Building an agreement: bottom-up or top-down?
9. Leadership: one leader or group consensus?
10. Risk taking: high or low?

In fact these differences span not only culture, but other types of interpersonal differences, such as gender and age. This chapter will look at how these ten differences can affect negotiation, and how you can bridge the gap.

1. Negotiating Goal: Contract or Relationship?

The first consideration has to do with whether or not the goal of the negotiation is a contract, a specific deal or outcome, or the formation of a relationship.

---

* Jeswald W. Salacuse, "Negotiating: The Top Ten Ways That Culture Can Affect Your Negotiation," *Ivey Business Journal*, Sept.–Oct. 2004; http://iveybusinessjournal.com/publication/negotiating-the-top-ten-ways-that-culture-can-affect-your-negotiation/.

In terms of cultural differences by nationality, Salacuse writes,

> Negotiators from different cultures may tend to view the purpose of a negotiation differently. For deal makers from some cultures, the goal of a business negotiation, first and foremost, is a signed contract between the parties. Other cultures tend to consider that the goal of a negotiation is not a signed contract but rather the creation of a relationship between the two sides. Although the written contract expresses the relationship, the essence of the deal is the relationship itself. For example, in my survey of over 400 persons from twelve nationalities, reported fully in *The Global Negotiator*, I found that whereas 74 percent of the Spanish respondents claimed their goal in a negotiation was a contract, only 33 percent of the Indian executives had a similar view. The difference in approach may explain why certain Asian negotiators, whose negotiating goal is often the creation of a relationship, tend to give more time and effort to negotiation preliminaries, while North Americans often want to rush through this first phase of deal making. The preliminaries of negotiation, in which the parties seek to get to know one another thoroughly, are a crucial foundation for a good business relationship. They may seem less important when the goal is merely a contract.

We can see this in terms of gender too. Women tend to be more relationship-focused; whereas, men tend to be more transactional. This means that when you're using the Everybody WINS method, you first need to examine your goal, and then the goal of the other person.

In some cases, it will be obvious. If you are negotiating the sale of a car, you're less likely to be concerned with building a relationship than you are in completing a transaction and getting a good deal on the contract. On the other hand, if you are negotiating with your boss, you may feel more like Antonio who is probably more concerned with maintaining a positive relationship with Mark.

Mark, on the other hand, being North American, is likely to not take a lot of time to consider Antonio's proposal.

2. Negotiating Attitude: Win-Lose or Win-Win?

In typical negotiations, there are two views. Either "we both win," or "we both lose." Of course, in this book, we've set forth a framework whereby Everybody WINS.

Salacuse writes, "As you enter negotiations, it is important to know which type of negotiator is sitting across the table from you. Here, too, my survey revealed significant differences among cultures. For example, whereas 100 percent of the Japanese respondents claimed that they approached negotiations as a win-win process, only 33 percent of the Spanish executives took that view."

When you are in the I phase of Everybody WINS, see if you can determine whether or not you are dealing with someone with a "win-lose" mindset. If so, you'll want to know this going in, so that you can frame your offer so that the other party will feel as if he or she "won."

3. Personal Style:
Informal or Formal?

This is another core area of interpersonal difference. Some negotiators are more informal, laid-back, and casual. Others are more formal and rigid. Salacuse writes,

> Personal style concerns the way a negotiator talks to others, uses titles, dresses, speaks, and interacts with other persons. Culture strongly influences the personal style of negotiators. It has been observed, for example, that Germans have a more formal style than Americans. A negotiator with a formal style insists on addressing counterparts by their titles, avoids personal anecdotes, and refrains from questions touching on the private or family life of members of the other negotiating team. A negotiator with an informal style tries to start the discussion on a first-name basis, quickly seeks to develop a personal, friendly relationship with the other team, and may take off his jacket and roll up his sleeves when deal making begins in earnest. Each culture has its own formalities with their own special meanings. They are another means of communication among the persons sharing that culture, another form of adhesive that binds them together as a community. For an American, calling someone by their first name is an act of friendship and therefore a good thing. For a Japanese, the use of the first name at a first meeting is an act of disrespect and therefore bad. Negotiators in foreign cultures must respect appropriate formalities. As a general rule, it is always safer to adopt a formal posture and move to an informal stance, if the situation warrants it, than to assume an informal style too quickly.

This is also an area that is affected by age. Younger people, such as millennials and Gen Xers, tend to be more casual than their older counterparts. When negotiating with someone from a different age group, it's important to be aware of the difference in formality.

As a general rule, it is always safer to adopt a formal posture and move to an informal stance, if the situation warrants it, than to assume an informal style too quickly.
—Jeswald Salacuse

4. Communication Style: Direct or Indirect?

Communication style differences play a huge part in negotiations. Salacuse writes,

In a culture that values directness, such as the American or the Israeli, you can expect to receive a clear and definite response to your proposals and questions. In cultures that rely on indirect communication, such as the Japanese, reaction to your proposals may be gained by interpreting seemingly vague comments, gestures, and other signs. What you will not receive at a first meeting is a definite commitment or rejection.

The confrontation of these styles of communication in the same negotiation can lead to friction. For example, the indirect ways Japanese negotiators express disapproval have often led foreign business executives to believe that their proposals were still under consideration when in fact the Japanese side had rejected them.

This is also an area where age and gender are relevant. As a general rule, younger people tend to be less direct than older people. And men tend to be more direct than women. This is also true with people who have status and power differences.

As in the case with Antonio, although he is a male, he is younger than Mark, and Mark is his boss, so there is a power and status difference; moreover, Antonio is from a culture that has more informal communication. This is what led Antonio to be too indirect in his first attempt at the email.

5. Sensitivity to Time: High or Low?

How urgent do you tend to regard things? That is the essence of this consideration. Salacuse writes,

> Discussions of national negotiating styles invariably treat a particular culture's attitudes toward time. It is said that Germans are always punctual, Latins are habitually late, Japanese negotiate slowly, and Americans are quick to make a deal. Commentators sometimes claim that some cultures value time more than others, but this observation may not be an accurate characterization of the situation. Rather, negotiators may value differently the amount of time devoted to and measured against the goal pursued. For Americans, the deal is a signed contract and time is money, so they want to make a deal quickly. Americans therefore try to reduce formalities to a minimum and get down to business quickly.

Japanese and other Asians, whose goal is to create a relationship rather than simply sign a contract, need to invest time in the negotiating process so that the parties can get to know one another well and determine whether they wish to embark on a long-term relationship. They may consider aggressive attempts to shorten the negotiating time as efforts to hide something.

In other words, time sensitivity in negotiation has more to do with whether or not you're developing a relationship or are conducting a transaction. So if you are trying to negotiate with someone with whom you value the relationship, you need to be more flexible with time.

6. Emotionalism: High or Low?

This consideration also has clear ramifications in negotiations. If you, or the other party, have a tendency to become highly emotional, then you can use this information to your strategic advantage. If it's you that gets emotional, plan a "cooling-down" strategy so that you can go to your balcony and keep the higher perspective.

If it's your opponent who tends to get emotional, make sure that you don't react or escalate. Salacuse writes,

Accounts of negotiating behavior in other cultures almost always point to a particular group's tendency to act emotionally. According to the stereotype, Latin Americans show their emotions at the negotiating table, while the Japanese and many other Asians hide their feelings. Obviously, individual personality plays a role here. There are passive Latins and hot-headed Japanese. Nonetheless, various cultures have different rules as to the appropriateness and form of displaying emotions, and these rules are brought to the negotiating table as well. Deal makers should seek to learn them.

In the author's survey, Latin Americans and the Spanish were the cultural groups that ranked themselves highest with respect to emotionalism in a clearly statistically significant fashion. Among Europeans, the Germans and English ranked as least emotional, while among Asians the Japanese held that position, but to a lesser degree.

Again, gender and age also influence this consideration. The stereotype is that women are more emotional than men and that both young people and old people tend to be more emotional than middle-aged people.

7. Form of Agreement: General or Specific?

This consideration has to do with the type of written agreement that is made after the negotiation. Some parties tend to want every little detail encapsulated in the agreement, while others are fine with more general ones.

Consider the divorcing couple, where the woman wants an inventory of all household items, and a calendar of visitation that extends ten years. The man, in this case, might not care about such a specific agreement, as long as he is getting "50 percent," whatever that means.

Age can be a factor here too. Younger people may have less experience than older ones. Older people have likely learned that unless one puts it in writing, there is no proof of agreement.

An interesting twist, though, lies in the idea that these differences might not have to do with gender, age, or culture, but with power differences.

Salacuse writes,

Cultural factors influence the form of the written agreement that the parties make. Generally, Americans prefer very detailed contracts that attempt to anticipate all possible circumstances and eventualities, no matter how unlikely. Why? Because the deal is the contract itself, and one must refer to the contract to handle new situations that may arise. Other cultures, such as the Chinese, prefer a contract in the form of general principles rather than detailed rules. Why? Because, it is claimed, the essence of the deal is the relationship between the parties. If unexpected circumstances arise, the parties should look primarily to their relationship, not the contract, to solve the problem. So, in some cases, a Chinese negotiator may interpret the American drive to stipulate all contingencies as evidence of a lack of confidence in the stability of the underlying relationship.

Among all respondents in my survey, 78 percent preferred specific agreements, while only 22 percent preferred general agreements. On the other hand, the degree of intensity of responses on the question varied considerably among cultural groups. While only 11 percent of the English favored general agreements, 45.5 percent of the Japanese and of the Germans claimed to do so.

Some experienced executives argue that differences over the form of an agreement are caused more by unequal bargain-

ing power between the parties than by culture. In a situation
of unequal bargaining power, the stronger party always seeks
a detailed agreement to "lock up the deal" in all its possible
dimensions, while the weaker party prefers a general agreement to give it room to "wiggle out" of adverse circumstances
that are bound to occur. According to this view, it is context,
not culture that determines this negotiating trait.

Whether the differences are due to gender, age, culture, relationship status, or power, one thing is clear. If in doubt, put it
in the written agreement.

If in doubt, put it in the written agreement.

---

8. Building an Agreement: Bottom-up or Top-down?

This has to do with how you structure the agreement. Do you
start with the specifics ("We want a 10 percent raise spread
out over the next three years") or do you start with the general areas of agreement and work down from there ("We want
a raise")? Salacuse writes,

> Some observers believe that the French prefer to begin with
> agreement on general principles, while Americans tend to
> seek agreement first on specifics. For Americans, negotiating
> a deal is basically making a series of compromises and trade-
> offs on a long list of particulars. For the French, the essence is

to agree on basic principles that will guide and indeed determine the negotiation process afterward. The agreed-upon general principles become the framework, the skeleton, upon which the contract is built.

My survey of negotiating styles found that the French, the Argentineans, and the Indians tended to view deal making as a top down (deductive) process; while the Japanese, the Mexicans and the Brazilians tended to see it as a bottom up (inductive) process. A further difference in negotiating style is seen in the dichotomy between the "building-down" approach and the "building-up approach." In the building-down approach, the negotiator begins by presenting the maximum deal if the other side accepts all the stated conditions. In the building-up approach, one side begins by proposing a minimum deal that can be broadened and increased as the other party accepts additional conditions. According to many observers, Americans tend to favor the building-down approach, while the Japanese tend to prefer the building-up style of negotiating a contract.

9. Leadership:
One Leader or Group Consensus?

This consideration relates to how many people it takes to make the decision to agree. Gender and age factor into this matter, as women tend to be more collaborative and relationship-oriented, as do older people. Young people and males tend to be more individualistic. According to Salacuse,

Culture is one important factor that affects how executives organize themselves to negotiate a deal. Some cultures emphasize the individual while others stress the group. These values may influence the organization of each side in a negotiation.

One extreme is the negotiating team with a supreme leader who has complete authority to decide all matters. Many American teams tend to follow this approach. Other cultures, notably the Japanese and the Chinese, stress team negotiation and consensus decision-making. When you negotiate with such a team, it may not be apparent who the leader is and who has the authority to commit the side. In the first type, the negotiating team is usually small; in the second it is often large. For example, in negotiations in China on a major deal, it would not be uncommon for the Americans to arrive at the table with three people and for the Chinese to show up with ten. Similarly, the one-leader team is usually prepared to make commitments more quickly than a negotiating team organized on the basis of consensus. As a result, the consensus type of organization usually takes more time to negotiate a deal.

10. Risk Taking: High or Low?

The final consideration for our purposes is that of risk aversion. Some people tend to be more risk-tolerant and others more risk-averse. While there are wide variations between people on this scale, the culture they were raised in does play a factor. Salacuse writes,

> In deal making, the negotiators' cultures can affect the willingness of one side to take risks—to divulge information, try new approaches, and tolerate uncertainties in a proposed

course of action. The Japanese, with their emphasis on requiring large amounts of information and their intricate group decision-making process, tend to be risk averse. Americans, by comparison, are risk takers.

Among all respondents in the survey, approximately 70 percent claimed a tendency toward risk taking while only 30 percent characterized themselves as low risk takers. Among cultures, the responses to this question showed significant variations. The Japanese are said to be highly risk averse in negotiations, and this tendency was affirmed by the survey which found Japanese respondents to be the most risk averse of the twelve cultures. Americans in the survey, by comparison, considered themselves to be risk takers, but an even higher percentage of the French, the British, and the Indians claimed to be risk takers.

Faced with a risk-averse counterpart, how should a deal maker proceed? The following are a few steps to consider:

1. Don't rush the negotiating process. A negotiation that is moving too fast for one of the parties only heightens that person's perception of the risks in the proposed deal.

2. Devote attention to proposing rules and mechanisms that will reduce the apparent risks in the deal for the other side.

3. Make sure that your counterpart has sufficient information about you, your company, and the proposed deal.

4. Focus your efforts on building a relationship and fostering trust between the parties.

5. Consider restructuring the deal so that the deal proceeds step by step in a series of increments, rather than all at once.

*   *   *

All of these considerations can be placed on continua. In other words, culture, gender, and age *do* factor into an individual's propensity to be high or low on these areas, but there are no hard-and-fast rules. It's about assessing your opponent in the negotiation and then modifying your behavior accordingly.

In the next chapter, we will wrap up the book with a look at some specific applications of the ideas you've learned.

12

Tips On **WIN**ning

In this chapter, we'll encapsulate and summarize how you can negotiate your way to the top with the Everybody WINS method.

Twelve Key Tips

Negotiating is the process of attempting to agree on a solution. Compromising, or settling on a mutually agreeable solution, is the result of successful negotiations. Compromise is all about being flexible. It means being able to generate alternate solutions when you've "hit the wall." Whether it involves a person you can't get along with, a change in office systems, a turf war that needs ending, or an idea you know will work but others are resisting, mastering the arts of negotiation and compromise are essential to your success. Here are twelve tips to keep in mind:*

---

* "Master the Negotiation: Twelve Tips for Negotiating and Compromising with Difficult People," Dale Carnegie Training, accessed Nov. 8, 2017; http://www.dalecarnegie.com/master-the-negotiation-12 -tips-for-negotiating-and-compromising-with-difficult-people/.

1. Have a positive attitude.

Your attitude is essential to the outcome. You have a much better chance of coming to an outcome involving mutual gains if you approach the negotiation as an opportunity to learn and achieve a win-win outcome.

2. Meet on mutual ground.

Find a mutually agreeable and convenient physical space to meet that is comfortable to all involved. Agree on when you will meet and on how much time is available to devote to the process. Whenever possible, deal with negotiations face-to-face. Be careful about using the phone and email. A lack of facial expressions, vocal intonation, and other cues can result in a negotiation breakdown.

3. Clearly define and agree on the issue.

Agree about the statement of the issue, using simple and factual terms. If the situation is multifaceted, search for ways to slice the large issue into smaller pieces, and deal with one issue at a time.

4. Do your homework.

Take time to plan. You must know not only what is at stake for you, but the other side's concerns and motivation as well. Take into consideration any history or past situations that might affect the negotiations. Know the must-haves (nonnegotiable items) and nice-to-haves (negotiable items). Determine the best resolution, a fair and reasonable deal, and a minimally acceptable deal.

5. Take an honest inventory of yourself.

Determine the level of trust in the other person and in the process. Be conscious of aspects of your personality that can help or hinder the process.

6. Look for shared interests.

Get on the same side by finding and establishing similarities. Conflict tends to magnify perceived differences and minimize similarities, so look for common goals, objectives, or even gripes that can show that you are in this together. Focus on the future, talk about what is to be done, and tackle the problem jointly.

7. Deal with facts, not emotions.

Address problems, not personalities. Avoid any tendency to attack the other person or to pass judgment on his or her ideas and opinions. Avoid focusing on the past or blaming the other person. Maintain a rational, goal-oriented frame of mind. This will depersonalize the conflict, separate the issues from the people involved, and prevent defensiveness.

8. Be honest.

Don't play games. Be honest and clear about what is important to you. It is equally important to be clear and to communicate why your goals, issues, and objectives are important to you.

9. Present alternatives and provide evidence.

Create options and alternatives that demonstrate willingness to compromise. Consider conceding in areas that might have high value to the other person but are not that important to you. Frame options in terms of the other person's interests and provide evidence for your point of view.

10. Be an expert communicator.
Nothing shows determination to find a mutually satisfactory resolution to conflict more than applying excellent communication skills. Ask questions, listen, rephrase what you heard to check for understanding, and take a genuine interest in the other side's concerns. Reduce tension through humor, let the other "vent," and acknowledge the other's views. Focus less on your position and more on ways in which you can move toward a resolution or compromise.

11. End on a good note.
Make a win-win proposal and check to make sure that everyone involved leaves the situation feeling they have won. Shake on it, agree on the action steps, who is responsible for each step, how success will be measured, and how and when the decision will be evaluated. Be open to reaching an impasse for noncritical issues: agree to disagree in these cases.

12. Enjoy the process.
Look at the benefits of learning other people's point of view. People report that after overcoming conflict and reaching an agreement, relationships have grown even stronger. Reflect and learn from each negotiation. Determine the criteria to evaluate the process and the solution.

Negotiation in Sales

Unless you have left yourself some leeway in your negotiations (that is, you started high so that you can negotiate down), stick to your guns on fees. Remember, you deserve to be compensated not only for the actual work, but for the months and years you've put into learning and practicing your craft. That time spent has value!

Your client needs to know that you're holding the winning hand. To put it another way, the client needs to be convinced that you have the power, through your talents, to bring about positive results for him through bigger donations, increased revenues, more online conversions, or whatever it may be. Some ways to attain that are these:

Never show weakness. Before going into negotiations, determine your own "Unique Value Proposition" (or a clear statement that describes what distinguishes you from the competition) and present yourself as being confident in your abilities. Don't be the first one to blink!

Show the client your skills and talents. Be ready to present similar projects you've done that have attained the results the client was looking for. If you don't have any similar projects, show existing examples of other documents and/or projects that mirror the direction you'd like to take.

Sell value, not services. An old sales aphorism says, "Sell the sizzle, not the steak." Remember, someone who buys a light bulb doesn't want the bulb; she wants the light it provides. A guy doesn't want a drill; he wants a hole through something. Keep your negotiations focused on the results your services will provide.

Listen and look for clues to the other party's real objections. Is it price? Is it lead time? Is it the prospect of losing his number-one customer? Read between the lines and get a handle on what your client is *not* saying for a look at what's really important to them.

Be ready to walk away. This is never easy, but is sometimes necessary. If you've done all you can to bring the deal to conclusion and your client is still asking for more, it's time to walk away. Sometimes your client will acquiesce, having tested you to see how far he could push. Or if she doesn't call you back to the table, take solace in the fact that you can move onto another project where you won't be simply trading time for dollars.

Negotiation in a Nutshell

Here's a quick summary of the main ideas that we've covered in this book.

Negotiation Best Practices

• Listen carefully.
• See the situation from the other person's perspective.
• Be confident.
• Be prepared.

- Don't be aggressive.
- Don't make it a formal process.
- Look for creative solutions.
- Understand what is important to the customer.
- Negotiate details before price.
- Recognize walk-away points.

Common Negotiation Mistakes

- Negotiating price before details
- Failing to keep the end in mind and leaving no room for negotiation
- Lack of confidence
- Failing to understand the needs of the customer
- Letting the customer dictate the process and outcomes
- Acting desperate
- Using argumentative communications
- Failing to recognize the walk-away points
- Narrowing negotiations to one point, usually price

Characteristics of a Great Negotiator

- Good reputation, with good intentions
- Respectful, trusting, and trustworthy
- Confident and positive
- Well-prepared
- Composed
- Effective communicator
- Good people skills
- Open-minded
- Creative
- Risk taker

Truths about Negotiation

- You do not have to be aggressive to be a good negotiator.
- Negotiating is not fighting.
- Most people have a natural talent for negotiation.
- You don't have to compromise your ethics to get what you want through negotiation.
- You don't have to have the upper hand to negotiate effectively.
- Negotiation is not always a formal process.
- There are no hard-and-fast rules to negotiation.
- Virtually everything that is a product of negotiation is negotiable.
- Expect customers to ask for a better deal.
- Learn to say no.
- Look for creative solutions to reach an agreement.

The Everybody WINS Worksheet

Negotiation is the process of creating an agreement that is an acceptable outcome for everybody.

Prior to the negotiation session(s), answer these questions as best as you can.

The issue being negotiated

_____

_____

_____

_____

_____

_____

W: Wait. This means to _wait_ until you've taken a look at your role in the negotiation, and have explored the environmental factors that are influencing it.

What is your pattern of decision making in this negotiation? (see chapter 1)

_____

_____

_____

What are some decision traps to watch out for? (see chapter 2)

_____

_____

_____

Are you a natural maximizer or satisficer? (see chapter 3)

_____

_____

_____

What is your primary conflict style? (see chapter 4)

_____

_____

_____

Whom are you negotiating with? (see chapter 5)

_____

_____

_____

What is your level of influence? (see chapter 5)

_____

_____

_____

When is the best time to have this negotiation? (see chapter 5)

_____

_____

_____

Where is the negotiation taking place? (see chapter 5)

_____

_____

_____

Why do you want to win? (see chapter 5)

_____

_____

_____

What is your desired outcome? (see chapter 5)

_____

_____

_____

Fill out the following list. For the first time, fill in *only* the "Item" and "Weight" columns. After initial discussions with the other party, you may want to come back to this list and fill out the "Adjusted" column if the value you're attaching to these items has changed.

What I Want in This Situation

Item	Weight	Weight Adjusted

I: Identify. This means to identify the elements in the other party that are relevant to the negotiation.

What is their pattern of decision making in this negotiation? (see chapter 2)

_____

_____

_____

What are some decision traps that the other side is falling into? (see chapter 2)

_____

_____

_____

Is the other party a natural maximizer or satisficer? (see chapter 3)

_____

_____

_____

What is their primary conflict style? (see chapter 4)

_____

_____

_____

What does the other party want? (see chapter 5)

_____

_____

_____

What are each party's interests and agendas or positions? (see chapters 5 and 6)

_____

_____

_____

Why do they want what they want? (see chapter 5)

_____

_____

_____

What are the barriers to cooperation? (see chapter 5)

_____

_____

_____

What is negotiable? (see chapter 5)

_____

_____

_____

What are some alternatives that might satisfy agendas and interests? (see chapter 5)

_____

_____

_____

N: Negotiate. This is the actual negotiation session or sessions. It's going back and forth with the other party until an acceptable outcome is established.

Value creation: what alternatives were generated? (see chapter 6)

_____

_____

_____

Value distribution: how will you frame your offer to convey maximized gains? (see chapter 7)

_____

_____

_____

S: Settle on an Agreement. This is coming up with the specific details of the agreement, as negotiated between the parties.

What are the specific details of the agreement? Write your notes here:

_____

_____

_____

_____

_____

_____

What are some things that could potentially derail the agreement?

_____

_____

_____

_____

_____

_____

13

Looking Ahead for the **WIN**

"Hello, this is NIA. How may I help you?"

"Yes, hi, this is Nancy. I received a letter regarding my student loans and was told to call this number."

"That's correct. This is the right number."

"Okay, good. So, I know that I haven't been able to keep up with my student loans, but I've had a good reason. Right after I graduated from college, I was diagnosed with cancer, and have been in and out of the hospital ever since."

"I understand. What you are saying is that you believe you have a valid medical reason to account for the delinquency, is that correct?"

"Yes, and if there were some way that I could get my loans forgiven, or at least reduced, it would really help me. I have so many medical expenses."

"So you wish to apply for student loan forgiveness or reduction?"

"Yes. Right now I can pay about $50 a month."

"Okay. Let's go over some options."

What Nancy does not know is that she is the only human being in this conversation. The other party, NIA, is actually an artificial intelligence chatbot, the Negotiation Intelligence Android. Although she is a fictional character created for the purposes of this book, technology is about to change the future of negotiation—for better and worse.

Here are some of the up-and-coming advances in technology as they relate to negotiation.

Artificial Intelligence

In June 2017, researchers at Facebook published an academic article describing an experiment they did in which they taught two artificial intelligence (AI) chatbots to negotiate with each other.*

In fact, AI negotiating is becoming so popular that there are competitions devoted to it, such as the International Automated Negotiating Agents Competition.**

While the idea of delegating negotiations to an AI agent is a long way off, the amount of research going on in that arena indicates that it's going to happen.

---

* Mike Lewis, Denis Yarats, et al., "Deal or No Deal? End-to-End Learning for Negotiation Dialogues," June 16, 2017; https://arxiv.org/pdf/1706.05125.pdf.

** See announcement for annual International Automated Negotiating Agents Competition, http://web.tuat.ac.jp/~katfuji/ANAC2017/.

Software Programs

Another area where technology is likely to affect negotiations is the development of negotiating software. Unlike AI, this is something that can actually affect the way everyday people negotiate.

With negotiation software, all of the proceedings take place in a shared platform.

Consultant David Wither puts it this way:*

> Everyone can add their own thoughts to proceedings and everyone can see who made what suggestion. Crucially, people can chip in with their intelligence without being in the room. That makes the negotiations far more informed than they would have been. The whole idea is to make it easy to organize your team, assign each team member to their parts of the negotiation, and to make sure everything is in order. Information can be centralized into one interactive dashboard. This way everyone knows what stage the negotiations are at and what needs to be done next. Facts can be checked and reputations can be inspected. This will improve the efficiency of your negotiating team and prevent negotiations from becoming bogged down.

The advantage of this is that the time-consuming back-and-forth, delays, and roadblocks are eliminated or minimized. Negotiations that used to take weeks can now be done in a few days.

---

* David Wither, "How Technology Is Changing the Face of Negotiation," *Huffington Post*, Oct. 5, 2016; http://www.huffingtonpost.com/entry/how-technology-is-changing-the-future-of-negotiation _us_57f48708e4b02d64cba52ed2.

VR Negotiation Training

Another up-and-coming way in which technology is changing negotiation is virtual-reality (VR) negotiation training, where you simulate a negotiation environment and use it to teach people how to negotiate more effectively.

Although the results at present only show improvement in communication skills and understanding of negotiation, with no significant results on outcome yet, this area is sure to continue to grow.* Perhaps the next training course you take will be in VR!

Texting

Finally, even text and instant messaging can affect the future of negotiations. Here is a humorous suggestion for some acronyms that could be used when negotiating by text, from Charles Dominick of Next Level Purchasing. Although this list is tongue-in-cheek and chiefly meant for purchasers, its suggestions could be useful in other contexts.**

2HI. "Too high": the supplier's price is too high: sent in reply to a supplier's text inquiring about the competitiveness of their offer.

BAFO. "Best and final offer," as in "send ur BAFO."

---

* Joost Broekens, Maaike Harbers, et al., "Virtual Reality Negotiation Training Increases Negotiation Knowledge and Skill," accessed Nov. 8, 2017; http://mmi.tudelft.nl/~joostb/files/Broekens%20et%20al%202012.pdf.

** Charles Dominick, "The Future of Negotiation: Texting?" Next Level Purchasing website, July 6, 2009; https://www.nextlevelpurchasing.com/blog/2009/07/the-future-of-negotiation-texting.html.

DL. "Deal," signifying that you've accepted the supplier's offer.

LTAS. "Leaning towards another supplier," sent in reply to a supplier's text asking about the status of your decision about their proposals. It is meant to compel the supplier to submit a revised, more attractive proposal.

SYP. "Sharpen your pencil," meaning, "Submit an offer more appealing to me."

Human Beings for the WIN

Regardless of the direction technology takes us in, one thing is for sure: nothing can replace the complex dynamic of two groups of people negotiating to come up with an agreement to solve a problem that they are all facing. It's a unique blend of mind, heart, body, and even soul.

The Everybody WINS process is among those negotiation methods that, once mastered, can really help make the world a better place. If more people cooperated in solving the problems that plague us, we'd have fewer social problems. And that, friends, is the real definition of a win.

CPSIA information can be obtained
at www.ICGtesting.com
Printed in the USA
JSHW052003100323
38811JS00001B/1